THE

APPLE RECIPE BOOK

ISBN 0 949089 04 4

© Copyright 1992 by
Southern Holdings Pty Ltd
Publishers
P.O. Huonville 7109
PHONE (002) 664112 FAX (002) 664112
Copies of this book are available from the publisher for $5.95 plus $1.60 p.& p.

A horsedrawn sled
carried spray in a barrel
with a hand pump in 1910.

When you bite into a crisp, juicy apple and enjoy its crunchy goodness and flavour, remember that not only are apples health-giving but also that the apple is 'Nature's toothbrush.' An apple, or even half an apple eaten at the end of a meal helps clean the teeth and mouth by removing particles of starchy and sugary foods, and by leaving an alkaline residue can help to reduce tooth decay.

orchard calendar

SPRING **September** **October**	Pruning is finished. Fertilizer is applied and trees are sprayed with fungicides to protect the new growth. Buds stir as the trees awake. Trees blossom, and fruit set takes place. Growers spray their trees to prevent fungus diseases.
November **SUMMER**	Trees are growing rapidly; orchards are leaf green again. Young fruitlets must be thinned out to avoid overloading the tree. Some colour is showing on the early varieties.
December **January**	Insects and fungus diseases must be sprayed regularly. As hot weather continues most growers have to irrigate their orchards so the fruit will grow big enough for market.
February **AUTUMN**	Harvest of early varieties continues. Water pipes with spray heads are linked between rows of trees to ensure maximum growth.
March	This is the main harvest period. Fruit is held in cold storage for sale later in the year.
April	Picking, sorting, grading and packing keep the grower busy. Harvesting continues as late varieties mature. Many itinerant pickers live in pickers huts or camp near the orchards.
May **WINTER** **June**	The apple harvest ends when late varieties are picked and put into cold storage. Growers now prepare their orchards for winter by cleaning drains and removing props and ladders. Leaves turn red and yellow, and begin to fall. By the end of June trees will be bare and dormant. The orchardist prunes his trees to remove unwanted growth and to control the crop for next season.
July	Pruning and training of trees continues. Fruit from cold stores is packed for sale. Ground between the trees is cultivated.
August	Young trees may be planted this month. Growers make sure that everything is in order for the new season, which will start in spring.

A load of 2,400 cases of apples from Huon ports for Hobart in 1914.

Grading and packing apples in a Franklin orchard.

contents

SALADS
1 Apple & Potato
1 Apple Jelly
1 Apple Salad
2 Crispy Salmon
2 Waldorf Salad
2 Apple Celery & Pineapple
3 Red Cabbage Toss
3 Sandwich Suggestions

MORNAYS & MEAT DISHES
4 Savoury Seasoning
4 Stuffed Pork Chops
4 Sweet & Sour Mornay
5 Sweet Curried Neck Chops
5 Curried Mince
6 Sausage Patties
6 Curried Sausage Casserole
7 Savoury Apple Pie
7 Curried Tuna & Mushroom
8 Seafood Casserole
8 Lamb & Apple Hotpot
9 Apple Cheese Tarts
9 Apple Stuffing
10 Savoury Stuffed Apples
10 Hot Apple Soup
11 Pork & Apple in foil
11 Savoury Pork Chops
12 Cider Pork Chops
12 Hamburgers
12 A quick Snack
13 Savoury Mince & Spaghetti
13 Sausage & Apple Bake
14 Curry Mornay
14 Apple Sauce
15 Apple Lamb Casserole

BISCUITS & SLICES
16 Apple Oat
16 Brownies
16 Apple & Raspberry

17 Fudge Squares
17 Apple & Bran Cookies
18 Viennese Slice
19 Apple Ginger Squares
19 Apple Buns
20 Little Apple Turnovers
20 Apple Drops
21 Golden Slice
21 Tasty Apple Muffins

PIES & TARTS
22 Apple Custard Pie
22 Old Fashioned Apple Pie
23 Lemon & Apple Tart
23 Apple Fruit Tart
24 Apple Slice
24 Crunch Top Apple Slice
25 Apple Blossom Pie

CAKES
25 Cinnamon Apple
26 German Coffee Slice
26 Apple Fruit Cake
27 Plain Apple
27 Apple Cake
28 Chocolate Apple
28 Cinnamon Apple
29 Sliced Apple Shortcake
29 Apple Cake
29 Upside Down Apple
30 Apple Fruit Cake
30 Loretta's Apple Cake
30 Apple Cream Slice
31 Caramel Ring
31 Apple Cake
31 Eggless Apple Cake
32 Apple Cheese Loaf
32 Apple Fruit Cake
33 Apple with Crumble Top
33 Boiled Fruit Cake

34 Apple Tea Cake
34 Eggless Apple Cake
34 Danish
35 Apple & Banana
35 Apple Filling
35 Apple Cake
36 Eggless Sandwich
36 Spiced Apple
36 Apple Nut
37 Quick Apple
37 Quick Apple Sponge
37 Apple Slice
38 Spiced Apple Cheese Cake
38 Little Apple Cakes
39 Apple Sauce Cake
39 Apple Nut Loaf
40 Chocolate Upside Down

COLD DESSERTS
40 Apple & Ginger Delight
41 Danish Apple Cake
41 Apple Parfait
42 Apple Mousse
42 Apple Snow
43 Apple Ice Cream
43 Apple Pyramid
44 Autumn Pudding

PUDDINGS
44 Apple & Raisin Pancakes
45 Apple Fritters
45 Apple Crunch
46 Apple & Date Crisp
46 Carrot & Apple
47 Quick Apple Streusel
47 French Apple Tart
47 Lazyman's Apple Pie
48 Apple Puffs
48 Novel Apple
48 Crunchy Apple & Banana
49 Quick Apple Dessert

49 Fruit Curls
49 Apple Roly Poly
50 Rice & Apple Custard
50 Apple & Rice Meringue
51 Apple Dumplings
51 Dutch Apple Pie
51 Apple Topping
52 Steamed Apple
52 Apple Sponge
52 Irish Apple Cake
53 Baked Apple Dessert
53 Apple Dessert Cake.
54 Delicious Apple Amber
54 Apple Bread & Butter
55 Apple Ginger Pudding
55 Apple Cottage Pudding
55 American Apple Dessert
56 Baked Apple Roll
56 Apple Puff
57 Apple Cobbler
57 Snowballs
57 Fried Apples
58 Apple Roly Poly
58 Apple Sponge
58 Sponge Top
59 Apple & Raisin Souffle
59 Apple & Lemon Crunch
60 Oslo Apple Cake
60 Apple Crumble
61 Apple Custard Cream Cake
61 Apple Honey Cake
62 Spiced Apple & Ginger
62 Apple Custard
63 Baked Apples
63 French Apple Pudding
64 Rosy Apples

JAMS
64 Apple Marmalade
64 Apple Jam

65 Apple & Orange
65 Apple Jelly
65 Apple Jam

SUNDRIES
66 Apple Chutney (1)
66 Apple Chutney (2)
67 Toffee Apples

67 Muesli
68 Simple Apple Muesli
68 Apple Cider (1)
68 Apple Cider (2)
69 Cinnamon Apple Slice
69 Butterscotch Dumplings
70 Popular Apple Varieties

Oven Temperature Guide

	Electric		Gas		
	°C	°F	°C	°F	Mark
Cool	110	225	100	200	1/4
Very Slow	120	250	120	250	1/2
Slow	150	300	150	300	1 - 2
Moderately Slow	170	340	160	325	3
Moderate	200	400	180	350	4
Moderately Hot	220	425	190	375	5 - 6
Hot	230	450	200	400	6 - 7
Very Hot	250	475	230	450	8 - 9

Measures

LIQUID		SOLID	
Imperial	Metric	Ounces	Grams
1 teaspoon	5ml	1oz	30g
1 tablespoon	20ml	4oz (1/4lb)	125g
2 fluid oz (1/4 cup)	62.5ml	8oz (1/2lb)	250g
4 fluid oz (1/2 cup)	125ml	12oz (3/4lb)	375g
8 fluid oz (1 cup)	250ml	16oz (1lb)	500g
1 pint (20 fluid oz/2-1/2 cups)	625ml	24oz (1-1/2lb)	750g
1 pint (US & Canada) (16 fluid oz)	500ml	32oz (2lb)	1kg

Cake Tins

6 inch - 15 cm
7 inch - 18 cm
9 inch - 23 cm

Loaf Tin: 9" x 5" - 23 x 12 cm
Bar Tin: 10" x 3" - 25 x 8 cm
Lamington: 11" x 7" - 28 x 18 cm

Apple trees in full blossom.

Drinking at the ford.

APPLE & POTATO SALAD

5 cold boiled potatoes, diced
1 apple, cored and chopped
1/2 cup mayonnaise
little finely chopped parsley
3 sticks celery chopped
salt and pepper to taste
little finely chopped mint
little finely chopped onion

Combine all ingredients, chill
and serve with lettuce, hard
boiled eggs and cold meat.

APPLE JELLY SALAD

2-3/4 cups apple juice heated
1 cup grated carrot
1/4 teaspoon salt
1/4 cup mayonnaise
2 packets lemon flavoured gelatine

2 tablespoons lemon juice
1/2 cup sliced celery
1/2 cup grated cucumber

Dissolve gelatine in hot apple juice and allow to cool.
Add remaining ingredients, stir until blended, pour into
mould, chill until firm. Serve with roast pork or chicken.

APPLE SALAD

2 red apples
2 green apples
grated carrot
125g diced matured cheese

juice of l/4 lemon
4 tablespoons chopped nuts
French dressing

Dice unpeeled apples and sprinkle with lemon juice.
Add all other ingredients and toss lightly.

WALDORF SALAD

1 green apple
1 red apple
juice of 1/2 lemon
1 cup finely chopped celery

1/2 cup chopped walnuts
1/2 cup mayonnaise
lettuce cups

Chill apples, core and dice, pour lemon juice over apples, add celery, walnuts and mayonnaise. Serve piled into lettuce cups.

CRISPY SALMON SALAD

1/2 cup mayonnaise
1/4 teaspoon salt
1/8 teaspoon pepper
2 tablespoons lemon juice
1 tablespoon grated onion
1/4 cup cream

1 small can salmon
1/4 cup sweet pickles
1/2 cup chopped celery
1 red apple
1 green apple

Blend salad dressing, salt, pepper, lemon juice, grated onion. Stir in lightly whipped cream, salmon, pickles, celery and diced apples. Chill thoroughly. Shape into moulds in lettuce cups and garnish with chopped parsley and crushed potato chips.

APPLE CELERY & PINEAPPLE SALAD

Combine 1 cup of chopped apple, 1 cup of chopped celery and a 450g (15 oz) tin of drained pineapple pieces together in a salad bowl. Squeeze over juice of 1/2 lemon, add 2 tablespoons of the pineapple juice and toss lightly.

* * * * * *
Add grated Granny Smith apple and 1 finely chopped onion to sausage mince when making sausage rolls.

RED CABBAGE & APPLE TOSS

1 small head red cabbage OR 1/2 large head finely shredded
2 tablespoons finely chopped onion

4 tablespoons salad oil	1 small green pepper
4 tablespoons vinegar	2 red eating apples
1 stalk celery	

Core apples (do not peel) and dice; slice green pepper. Combine cabbage, celery, apples and onion in bowl; sprinkle with salt. Combine remaining ingredients and mix well, then chill 1 hour before serving.

* * * * * *

For longer keeping, STORE apples in the lower section of the refrigerator..

SANDWICH SUGGESTIONS

1. Lettuce, chopped apple and chopped nuts.
2. Grate apple, mix with chopped nuts and beat with the butter.
3. Chop 2 apples. Wash and chop 4 sticks celery. Mix together with 2 tablespoons mayonnaise.
4. Grated apple mixed with honey and chopped nuts.
5. Chopped apple and celery mixed with peanut paste.

3

SAVOURY SEASONING FOR POULTRY

Mix freshly made breadcrumbs with 1 grated onion, 1 grated apple, pinch of mixed herbs, pinch of thyme, salt and pepper. Add a little water, or 1 egg if mixture is too dry.

STUFFED PORK CHOPS

4 level tablespoons dripping or lard
1 thick loin chop for each person
pepper, salt, little flour
2 tablespoons sugar

1 level tablespoon butter
2 tablespoons sugar
500g cooking apples

Wipe meat with damp cloth and with sharp knife cut slit in each. Fill cavity with apple sauce made by putting into a saucepan peeled, cored and sliced apples with sugar, butter and very little water if necessary, and cook until tender. Sew or skewer firmly the opening, dredge chops with flour and place in hot fat in a baking dish. Sprinkle with salt and pepper and roast gently for 3/4 hour, turning when half cooked. Serve with brown gravy and the remainder of the apple sauce.

SWEET & SOUR MORNAY

750g (1-1/2 lb) baby veal (diced)
1 tablespoon soya sauce
seasoning to taste
1 small tin pineapple pieces
2-1/2 cups stock (2 or 3 chicken cubes)

1 large onion
3/4 cup sultanas
1/2 cup rice
2 apples diced

Brown veal in frypan with a teaspoon of margarine and fry onion. Place in a large saucepan water, sultanas, apples, soya sauce, pineapple pieces and season to taste, then add browned veal and onion. Simmer for 1-1/2 hours, then add cooked rice. Thicken, place in casserole, top with breadcrumbs and grated cheese. Reheat.

SWEET CURRIED NECK CHOPS

1 large chopped onion
2 level tablespoons flour
2 level tablespoons dripping
1 level tablespoon curry powder
2 level tablespoons brown sugar
3 cups beef or chicken soup (stock)
lemon wedges and parsley to garnish

6 lamb chops
1 chopped apple
1 level teaspoon salt
juice of 1/2 lemon
seasoned flour
1/4 cup sultanas

Trim excess fat and gristle from chops. Toss in seasoned flour and fry for 15 minutes. Drain well. Prepare sauce by frying chopped apple and onion in extra dripping until lightly browned. Add flour, curry powder, brown sugar and salt, cook for 1 minute. Add stock and stir until sauce boils and thickens, then add lemon juice and sultanas. Add chops, place lid on saucepan and simmer gently for 30 minutes. Garnish with lemon wedges and parsley.

CURRIED MINCE

500g minced steak
1 cooking apple
1 medium onion
1 tablespoon marg or oil
1 tablespoon plum jam or chutney
1 dessertspoon curry powder

2 tablespoons flour
salt
1 cup water (approx)
1 lemon peel

Peel, core and slice apples and onions. Brown in margarine. Add meat, brown well. Add other ingredients, stir until boiling. Simmer for 20 minutes, adding more water if necessary.

SAUSAGE PATTIES WITH APPLE RINGS

500g sausage mince   butter
2 large cooking apples   flour

Shape mince into 8 flat patties and coat with flour. Wash
apples and remove cores. Slice each thickly (4 slices
each). Fry patties and apple rings in butter in frypan.
Serve immediately with green peas and creamy mashed
potato, onion rings can be fried and served if liked.

EASY CURRIED SAUSAGE CASSEROLE

750g (1-1/2 lb) sausages   2 tablespoons oil
1 cup diced mixed vegies   1 cup water
1 medium onion, sliced   cup sultanas
2 tablespoons fruit chutney   1 pkt curry sauce mix
1 medium apple, peeled, cored and sliced.

Pre-heat oven to 190 deg(c), 375 deg(f). Gently fry
sausages in heated oil until golden brown. Drain
and place in casserole. Add mixed vegetables, onion
apple sultanas and chutney. Blend sauce with water
and pour over sausages and vegetables. Cover and
cook in oven until sausages are cooked through -
about 45 minutes. Serve with boiled rice.

* * * * * *

For a change - add a grated apple
to your favourite hamburger mixture.

SAVOURY APPLE PIE

500g sausage meat
125g bacon
2 granny smith apples
3 tomatoes
4 level tablespoons finely grated cheese

1 level tablespoon butter
1 tablespoon chopped parsley
1 kg cooked, mashed potato
4 level tablespoons flour

Cook and mash potato, add butter, flour, salt and pepper. Knead well until a thick paste. Put half in a pie plate, line base and sides. Cover with layer of sausage meat, then sliced apple, tomato and more apple. Chop bacon and put a layer then sliced tomato. Cover with the other half mashed potato mixture, cover with grated cheese. Bake in hot oven 40 - 45 minutes.

CURRIED TUNA & MUSHROOM MORNAY

470g (15 oz) chunk style tuna
1 dessertspoon sugar
2 cups stock or water
1 tablespoon flour
1/2 teaspoon pepper
1 dessertspoon curry powder
1 dessertspoon chutney

250g (8oz) can mushrooms
2 sliced onions
1 teaspoon salt
1 dessertspoon sultanas
1 teaspoon margarine
1 small apple

Melt margarine in frypan, add onion and apple, then fry until light brown. Stir in flour, curry powder, sugar and seasonings and cook for 1 minute. Add stock and stir until mixture boils, add tuna, mushrooms, chutney and sultanas. Nice served with boiled rice.

* * * * *

Add a chopped red apple, with skin, to a coleslaw.

*Add a whole, cored apple per person
to the roast (especially nice with roast pork).*

SEAFOOD CASSEROLE

1 apple (chopped)
1 onion (chopped)
1/2 cup celery (chopped)
2 level tablespoons margarine
1 dessertspoon sultanas
1 pkt dutch curry & rice soup, pinch salt & pepper

1 large tin tuna
little lemon juice
little chopped green pepper
475ml water

Melt fat in large saucepan, lightly fry onion, apple and celery, add soup mix and stir well. Blend in water gradually. Cover and simmer slowly 15 minutes. Stir occasionally. Fold in other ingredients. Heat thoroughly. Serve with boiled rice. (A good deep freeze stand-by)

LAMB & APPLE HOT POT

6 lamb neck chops
1 tablespoon oil
2 onions
2 apples

3 tomatoes
1 cup beef stock
chopped parsley

Place chops in casserole dish, cover and cook at 350 deg. for 1 hour. Cut onion rings and apple rings, skin tomatoes and cut in halves, saute vegetables and fruit in oil. Strain fat from chops, add apples, vegetables and stock, cover and return to oven for 20 - 30 minutes. Thicken if desired and sprinkle with parsley.

APPLE CHEESE TARTS

2 cups plain flour   1/2 teaspoon salt
1 teaspoon baking powder   water

Sift flour and salt, rub in butter, add baking powder, mix to stiff dough with egg yolk and cold water, line patty tins.

FILLING

4 cooking apples   2 eggs
4 tablespoons melted butter   1/2 cup chopped walnuts
1/4 cup sugar   1 cup finely grated cheese

Steam and mash apples, add butter, sugar, half cheese and well beaten eggs. Fill lined patty tins, sprinkle with grated cheese and walnuts. Bake at 450 deg. until filling is set and pastry brown.

APPLE STUFFING

2 cups tart apples (chopped)   1/4 cup brown sugar
2 teaspoons grated lemon peel   5 cups bread crumbs
cup seedless raisins   1/2 cup chopped prunes
4 tablespoons butter (melted)   1/2 teaspoon cinnamon
1/2 teaspoon sweet paprika   3/4 teaspoon salt
1/4 cup apple juice.

Rub cavity of bird with 1/2 lemon, combine all ingredients, mix well, use to stuff chicken, turkey, duck or loin of pork.

* * * * *

Add a grated granny smith apple to your favourite stuffing when roasting chicken, or add 1 whole peeled apple and 1 small onion instead of stuffing in poultry.

SAVOURY STUFFED APPLES

1 cup soft breadcrumbs	6 red apples
8 prunes, pitted & chopped	grated rind 1/2 lemon
1/8 teaspoon ground cinnamon	1/2 teaspoon brown sugar
3 tablespoons melted butter	1 small egg (beaten)
2 tablespoons chopped walnuts	

Wash and dry apples, peel and strip off skin from top of each apple. Remove cores and scoop out some of the apple flesh. Chop the flesh and mix with breadcrumbs. Add prunes, walnuts, lemon rind, sugar, cinnamon and 2 tablespoons of the butter. Season to taste with salt, and bind with beaten egg.

Place each apple on a square of alfoil, bringing foil up around sides of apple to form a small cup. Fill centres generously with stuffing and brush tops with remaining butter.

Cook in oven 375 deg. for 1 hour. Serve with roast pork.

HOT APPLE SOUP

2 tablespoons butter	1/8 teaspoon ginger
2 tablespoons diced onion	1/8 teaspoon mace
500g apples, unpeeled	1 tablespoon flour
1 cup water	1 cup pineapple juice

Melt butter in saucepan, add onion and cook for 2 minutes. Core and cut apples, place in saucepan with water, ginger, mace; cover and bring to boil.

Cook 5 minutes. Pour in blender, add flour, blend until smooth. Add pineapple, reheat, boil 5 minutes. Adjust seasoning, serve with crisp cheese croutons.

PORK & APPLE IN FOIL

4 large pork chops   2 cooking apples & 1 orange
4 sage leaves OR 1/4 teaspoon dried sage; oil, salt, pepper

Brown chops quickly in frypan to which a very little oil has
been added to prevent them sticking. Season with salt and
pepper. Cut four pieces of aluminium foil about 10 inches
square. Rub a little oil on the foil and place one chop on
each square. Peel and core the apples, slice thickly and
divide into four equal portions. Place on top of the chops.
Place one fresh sage leaf or a pinch of dried sage on the
apples. Finely grate orange rind and sprinkle over the sliced
apples. Sprinkle a little orange juice on each serving before
parcelling it loosely. Place the parcels on a baking tray and
cook for about an hour in a moderate oven. Potatoes can
also be cooked in foil at the same time.

SAVOURY PORK CHOPS WITH APPLES

1 tablespoon chopped parsley   500g (1 lb) apples
a little butter   1 tablespoon sugar
juice of 1 lemon   salt and pepper
about 1/2 cup red wine   1 egg & a little milk
soft breadcrumbs   4 small pork chops
1 tablespoon chopped onion   fat for frying
1 teaspoon chopped sage OR pinch of herbs

Mix together the onion, parsley, sage or herbs, seasonings,
egg and milk. Beat lightly and put onto a plate. Put the
trimmed chops into this mixture and leave 15 minutes,
turning occasionally. Drain and dip into soft breadcrumbs.
Fry in a little hot fat until brown and continue cooking slowly
about 15 minutes. Peel, slice and simmer apples with butter,
sugar, lemon juice and red wine until tender. Serve the apple
with the pork chops.

CIDER PORK CHOPS

6 - 8 pork chops
salt and pepper
plain flour
3 - 4 onions

parsley
1/2 cup apple cider
1/4 cup water
2 apples

Trim fat from chops and heat trimmings in a frypan until fat starts to run. Then add chops, seasoned and coated with flour. Fry on both sides until browned. Place chops in casserole, add onions to frypan and cook until golden. Turn onions on to chops in casserole, add chopped parsley, cider and water.
Peel, core and slice apples on to top of chops.
Cover and bake in oven 375 deg. for 1-1/2 to 2 hours.
Serve with mashed potatoes and peas or fluffy boiled rice.

HAMBURGERS

500g minced steak
1 cup Easi oats
1 med. onion chopped finely
1 small cooking apple, grated

1/2 cup milk
1 teaspoon salt
1/2 teaspoon pepper
1 egg

Combine all ingredients in a large bowl. Shape into patties of desired size. Cook in oiled frypan over medium heat until done.

A QUICK SNACK

Sufficient slices of bread for each person.
Butter and place on them thin slices of apple, bananas, bacon and top with cheese. Bake in moderate oven for 20 - 30 minutes.

SAVOURY MINCE & SPAGHETTI

250g unoooked spaghetti   500g minced steak
1 450g can tomato soup   2 large onions, chopped
cup grated matured cheese   30g margarine
1 cup chopped carrots   1 cup sliced green beans
1 cup peeled & chopped cooking apples

Lightly fry the onions in the margarine; add the minced
steak and stir until brown. Add the prepared vegetables,
apple and some water. Simmer gently until tender, add
the tomato soup.
Cook the spaghetti in plenty of boiling water until tender.
Drain and add to the mixture. Place in an ovenproof dish,
sprinkle with the grated cheese, and brown in a moderate
oven for about 1/2 hour.

SAUSAGE & APPLE BAKE

1 tablespoon dripping   1 beef cube
125g streaky bacon   150 ml hot water
1 - 2 cooking apples
500g pork sausages or patties made of sausage meat

Melt fat and quickly brown sausages or patties.
Remove rinds from bacon and wrap each sausage in half
a rasher. Pack side by side in a casserole just big enough
to hold them. Peel and core apples and slice in rings.
Place on top of sausages. Crumble stock cube, dissolve
in water, pour over sausages. Cover and bake in moderate
to hot oven for 30 minutes or until bacon and apples are
cooked. Serves 4.

* * * * * *

Add an apple to your favourite curry

13

CURRY MORNAY

2 tablespoons tomato sauce	750g minced meat
1 dessertspoon coconut	1 onion (large)
1 dessertspoon curry powder	2 apples
1 tablespoon margarine	1/2 cup sultanas
1 tablespoon soya sauce	season to taste
1/2 small tin crushed pineapple	

Fry onion, mince and margarine and brown well or until fat is dissolved. Prepare apple by cutting into small pieces, pineapple, coconut, tomato sauce, soya sauce, sultanas and place in a large saucepan. Add 2-1/2 cups of stock OR water. Add 2 large beef cubes. Put mince mixture into saucepan after browning and simmer for 1-1/2 hours. Thicken. Place in casserole to cool, then top with breadcrumbs and grated cheese, reheat for use. (This is better made a few hours before eating).

APPLE SAUCE

To serve with pork, duck, pork sausages, etc.

3 cooking apples	sugar to taste
3 tablespoons water	1 teaspoon lemon juice
pinch cinnamon or a clove	1 tablespoon shortening

Peel and core apples. Cook with the shortening, water and flavourings until tender. Remove the clove, if used. Puree until smooth and add sugar to taste.

APPLE LAMB CASSEROLE

1 bayleaf
2 cups water
1 teaspoon salt
2 tablespoons plain flour
500g lamb shoulder (cubed)
pinch thyme, sage OR rosemary
3 cups apples, peeled and sliced

1 cup water
1 small onion
2 tablespoons sugar
pepper to taste
2 tablespoons lemon juice
2 level tablespoons butter

SCONE TOPPING
1-1/2 cups S.R. flour
1/3 cup milk
1/2 teaspoon curry powder
57g (2 oz) butter

1 egg
1/2 teaspoon turmeric
1/2 teaspoon salt

Melt butter in pan, add lamb and brown well. Sprinkle with flour, stir and coat meat, then stir in 2 cups water, bayleaf, salt, thyme, sage, pepper and onion. Cover and cook 1-1/2 hours until meat is tender. Stir occasionally. Remove bayleaf and onion. Prepare sliced apples and sprinkle with lemon juice. Add 1 cup water, sugar and apple to meat mixture. Cook, stirring occasionally until apples are tender, about 15-20 minutes. Turn on to a shallow baking dish. Top hot mixture with scone topping. Bake in hot oven for 12 - 15 minutes.

SCONE TOPPING
Sift together flour, turmeric, salt and curry powder into mixing bowl. Cut in butter. Combine egg, milk and add to dry ingredients. Mix lightly and knead on floured board. Roll on to 2 thickness and cut with round cutter into 2 inch circles.

* * * * * *

Apples, cheese and crisp biscuits make excellent party fare.

APPLE OAT BISCUITS

2 eggs
1/2 cup butter
1 cup S.R. flour
2/3 cup brown sugar
1 cup chopped apple

1/2 teaspoon salt
1/2 teaspoon nutmeg
1 teaspoon cinnamon
1 cup chopped walnuts
1 cup quick cooking oats

Cream butter and sugar well, add eggs one at a time, beating well. Add sifted flour and spices, and lastly the apple, oats and nuts. Drop teaspoonfulls onto a greased tray and bake in moderate oven approximately 15 minutes.

APPLE BROWNIES

1 cup raw apples (finely chopped)
2/3 cup margarine
2 cups brown sugar
1/2 cup chopped nuts

a pinch of salt
2 cups S.R. flour
1 teaspoon vanilla
2 eggs (beaten)

Cream butter, sugar, eggs and vanilla. Add flour, apple, nuts and mix well. Turn into greased 9" x 13" baking dish and place in moderate oven for 30-35 minutes.
Cool and cut into bars.

APPLE & RASPBERRY TART

1 egg
1/2 cup castor sugar
3/4 cup flour

1 teaspoon vanilla
113g (4oz) butter

3 apples cooked, mashed and sweetened; add 1/2 cup of raspberries or 3 tablespoonfuls of raspberry jam. Cream butter and sugar, add egg and vanilla, sift in flour and baking powder to shortbread consistency, press 2/3 into a 9" tin, the other 1/3 place in the fridge for 1/2 hour.
Mix apple and berries or jam, spread over pastry.
Crumble or grate 1/3 from fridge over top and bake 370 deg. for 30 minutes.

APPLE FUDGE SQUARES

1 cup sugar
1/2 cup margarine
2 eggs well beaten
2/3 cup stewed apples
1/2 teaspoon baking powder
57g (2 oz) unsweetened chocolate

pinch salt
1 cup sifted flour
1/2 cup chopped nuts
1 teaspoon vanilla
1/4 teaspoon carb. soda

Melt chocolate and margarine. Blend eggs, stewed apple and vanilla. Sift together flour, sugar, baking powder, soda and salt; stir into chocolate mixture. Stir in nuts. Spread in greased 8" x 8" pan and bake at 350 degrees for 30 - 40 minutes. Cut into squares.

APPLE & BRAN COOKIES

1-3/4 cups flour
1/2 teaspoon salt
1/2 cup shortening
1/2 teaspoon powdered cloves
1/2 teaspoon nutmeg
1 cup sweetened stewed apple

1 egg
1 cup sugar
1 cup raisins
1 teaspoon baking soda
1 teaspoon cinnamon
1 cup bran flakes

Sift flour, salt and spices. Cream shortening, add sugar gradually. Beat until light and fluffy, add egg. Combine soda and stewed apple. Add to creamed mixture alternately with dry ingredients. Add raisins and bran and blend well. Drop by teaspoons on to greased baking tray and cook at 375 deg. for 10 - 15 minutes.

VIENNESE APPLE SLICE

1/3 cup milk
1 tablespoon rum (optional)
1 teaspoon cinnamon
4-6 oz (125g-185g) cooking chocolate
8" x 4" x 1/2" (20cm x lOcm x 1.2cm) plain cake

PASTRY

1 dessertspoon water
1 teaspoon grated lemon rind
1 dessertspoon rum (optional)
3 tablespoons ground almonds
1-1/2 tablespoons castor sugar

pinch salt
1 egg yolk
1 cup plain flour
3 oz (90g) butter

PASTRY METHOD

Sift flour, salt and sugar, rub in butter. Stir in ground almonds and lemon rind. Combine egg yolk, water and rum. Stir in dry ingredients.
Knead well. Refrigerate at least 30 minutes.

APPLE MIXTURE METHOD

Peel, core and slice apples. Bring water and sugar to boil, add apples and cook until tender, not soft. Cool.

METHOD TO MAKE CAKE

Mix together rum, milk and cinnamon. Sprinkle over cake. Roll out pastry on well floured board to 8" X 12" (20cm X 30cm). Place cake in centre of pastry, pile apple on cake. Seal edges. Place on greased tray. Bake in moderate oven 25 minutes or until golden. Loosen and cool on tray. When cool coat with melted chocolate.
This is a cake for special occasions, but well worth the extra effort.

APPLE GINGER SQUARES

BASE
1 cup flour
1 egg , 1-1/4 cups water
1 teaspoon ginger
5 tablespoons butter
3 tablespoons treacle
1 teaspoon mixed spice
1 teaspoon baking soda
3 tablespoons golden syrup

TOPPING
1/2 cup sultanas
1 tablespoon sugar
2 tablespoons butter
2 tablespoons chopped nuts
5 apples peeled and sliced
2 tablespoons finely chopped
   peel

Sift ingredients. Melt butter, treacle and syrup, add egg and water. Pour onto dry ingredients, mix well. Turn into 8" tin lined with greased paper. Bake at 375 deg. for 20 minutes. Turn onto sugared paper, place on square serving plate and cover with hot topping.

TOPPING
Melt butter, add remaining ingredients, cover and cook to a pulp. Serve with sprinkling of cinnamon and sugar.

APPLE BUNS

1/2 cup brown sugar
1 pkt frozen bread rolls
1 lb (454g) stewed apples
1/2 teaspoon ground ginger
4 oz (ll3g) butter or substitute.

1 egg
sugar
1 cup sultanas
1 teaspoon cinnamon

Thaw bread rolls. Cream butter and sugar, add apples, sultanas, ginger and cinnamon, mix well. Roll out each bread roll to 7" diameter. Put a heaped tablespoon of mixture in centre of each circle. Bring sides of dough up around filling, squeeze dough together lightly over filling to give a haversack shape. Put on greased oven tray, brush rolls with lightly beaten egg, sprinkle with sugar.
Bake in moderate oven 20 minutes.

LITTLE APPLE TURNOVERS

SHORT PASTRY

pinch salt
1 egg yolk
8 oz (227g) flour
6 oz (170g) butter

1/2 teaspoon lemon juice
2 oz (57g) castor sugar
3 tablespoons thick sour cream

Sift flour with salt and sugar, cut butter into it, add egg yolk, cream and lemon juice, form into stiff dough. Cover and stand 1 hour before use.

FILLING

1 tablespoon rum
4 apples, peeled, quartered
4 oz (113g) castor sugar

1 egg yolk
1 tablespoon milk

Mix rum and sugar, pour over apples and leave to stand 1 hour. Roll dough, cut into 16 squares, put 1 apple quarter on each square, draw up corners and press together. Arrange on buttered, floured baking tray, brush with egg and milk. Bake in hot oven for 20 - 30 minutes. Dust with vanilla sugar; serve hot or cold.

APPLE DROPS

1 teaspoon salt
4 oz (113g) butter
1/2 teaspoon nutmeg
1 teaspoon carb. soda
1 teaspoon cinnamon
1/2 cup chopped nuts

1 egg
1/4 cup milk
2-1/2 cups plain flour
1-1/2 cups brown sugar
1/4 teaspoon ground cloves
2 cups finely chopped peeled apples

Cream butter, sugar and spices. To the creamed mixture add sifted flour, carb. soda and egg. Stir in apple, nuts and milk. Place dessertspoons of mixture on tray. Bake in hot oven 10 - 12 minutes. Ice while warm.

GOLDEN SLICE

3 oz (85g) sugar
3 oz (85g) copha
2 cups self raising flour

1 egg
pinch salt

Place sugar, egg, salt and half of the flour into bowl. Melt copha over low heat and add to dry ingredients. Beat well, about two minutes. Add remaining sifted flour and mix to firm dough. Roll out and line lamington tin.

TOPPING

1/4 cup coconut
1 cup apple pulp
12 oz (340g) stale cake crumbs
extra castor sugar and cinnamon

2 teaspoons cinnamon
1/4 cup chopped walnuts
few drops almond essence
1 tablespoon golden syrup

Combine cake crumbs, coconut, apple pulp, syrup, cinnamon, almond essence and half the walnuts. Press together with fingers until well combined. Press this mixture over pastry, sprinkle top with extra sugar and cinnamon and remaining walnuts. Bake in moderate-hot oven 30-35 minutes. Cut into slices. Allow to cool in tin.

TASTY APPLE MUFFINS

1/2 teaspoon salt
2 cups self raising flour
4 tablespoons sugar
1 teaspoon cinnamon

1 egg
1 cup milk
1 cup grated apple
1/2 cup melted margarine

Sift flour, salt, sugar and cinnamon. Add milk and beaten egg, mix lightly then stir in the melted margarine and the grated apple. Mix thoroughly and pour into greased muffin tins filling them 2/3 full. Bake in oven 400 deg. for 15-20 minutes.

APPLE CUSTARD PIE

1 teaspoon cinnamon   1/2 cup water
8 tart apples peeled & cored   3/4 cup sugar
grated peel & juice of one lemon 1/4 teaspoon nutmeg

Boil these ingredients until apples are soft, let cool, beat
2 eggs with 1/4 cup of melted butter, add to apple mix,
beat well, then put through sieve, bake in pie shell 30-40
minutes. Serve with whipped cream or ice cream.

OLD FASHIONED APPLE PIE

squeeze of lemon juice   1/3 cup sugar
4 large cooking apples (about 2 lbs)
Stew apples until soft with very little water and sugar
and lemon juice.

1 oz (28g) sugar   1 egg
4 oz (ll3g) butter   4 tablespoons milk
8 oz (227g) self raising flour

Cream butter and sugar, then beat in egg and add sifted
flour and milk alternately. Mix to a soft dough and divide
into two. Roll pastry between two sheets of plastic film as
it is very soft, and use half to line a tart plate. Fill with
warm-hot apple and cover with remainder of pastry.
Decorate and sprinkle with castor sugar. Bake in moderate
oven (370-400 deg.) for 30-40 minutes.

LEMON & APPLE TART

1 egg   1 apple
rind & juice of 1 lemon   1/2 cup sugar
piece of butter (size of walnut)

Cream butter and sugar, add grated rind and juice of
one lemon. Add grated apple and beaten egg. Pour into
uncooked pastry case. Cook at 400 deg. for about 20
minutes.

APPLE FRUIT TART

PASTRY

4 oz (ll3g) sugar   1 egg
8 oz (227g) butter   pinch salt
1 lb (454g) plain flour   1 tablespoon cinnamon
1 teaspoon baking powder

Sift the flour, cinnamon, baking powder and salt into
a bowl and rub in butter until mixture resembles bread
crumbs. Add the sugar and beaten egg and knead until
all the flour has been mixed. Roll out and line a greased
8" tin.

FILLING

6 oz (170g) sugar   2 oz (57g) butter
4 oz (113g) raisins   1 teaspoon cinnamon
1 lb (454g) cooking apples

Boil until mixture is brown and fairly dry. Fill the pastry
shell and cover with another layer of pastry.
Cook in moderate oven.

APPLE SLICE

PASTRY

cup plain flour
1 tablespoon sugar
2-3 tablespoons cold water

pinch salt
1 cup self raising flour
3 oz (85g) butter

Rub butter into sifted flour and salt, add sugar, then water to make stiff dough.

CAKE TOPPING

2 eggs
4 oz (113g) butter
1 cup self raising flour

3/4 cup sugar
1/2 cup plain flour
1 tablespoon lemon juice

Cream butter and sugar, add eggs, lemon juice and sifted flours. Put pastry into a lamington tin, then spread with fairly dry stewed apple and then the cake topping. Cake topping must be fairly stiff and should be spread on top with a fork or fingers. Bake in hot oven for 10 minutes (475 deg.) then moderate oven for 30-40 minutes (440 deg.). When cool, ice with lemon or vanilla icing.

CRUNCH TOP APPLE SLICE

1 cup raisins
1 teaspoon nutmeg
1 teaspoon vanilla
1-1/2 teaspoons cinnamon
pinch powdered cloves
1/4 cup chopped walnuts

pinch salt
1 cup sugar
1/2 cup margarine
2 cups S.R. flour
1 teaspoon carb. soda

1 cup unsweetened stewed apple (drained)

Cream butter, sugar, add stewed apple, then remaining ingredients. Spread in a swiss roll tin.

Combine: 2/3 cup crushed cornflakes, 1/4 cup sugar, 1/4 cup walnuts (chopped), 2 tablespoons of softened margarine. Sprinkle over base and bake in moderate oven 30 minutes. Cool and cut into bars.

APPLE BLOSSOM PIE

biscuit pastry   1 baked pastry case of shortcrust
crumb or cornflake shell

FIRST LAYER

2 or 3 apples   1/4 cup sugar
1/2 cup sugar   pulp of 2 passion fruit

SECOND LAYER

1 egg yolk   juice of 1 lemon
1/2 tin sweetened condensed milk

THIRD LAYER

whipped cream   1 egg white
1 dessertspoon gelatine   1/2 teaspoon lemon essence
juice drained from stewed apple made up to 3/4 cup of liquid.
Stew apples, add juice of lemon & passion fruit. When cool
put in pastry case. Mix ingredients of 2nd layer and spread
on top of apples. For the topping, dissolve the gelatine in
the hot syrup, add essence and allow to set lightly. Add a
pinch of salt to egg white and beat till stiff, colour pale pink,
gradually add the partially set apple mixture and continue
beating until thick. Pile on top of other layers and decorate
with whipped cream.

CINNAMON APPLE CAKE

1/2 cup sugar   1 egg
1 tablespoon cinnamon   1 cup S.R. flour
about 2 lbs (909g) apples   3oz (90g) butter
Stew, drain apples, keeping hot. Cream butter & sugar and
beat in egg. Stir in sifted flour, cinnamon and pinch of salt.
Put half mixture into sponge sandwich tin or pie plate, bringing mixture up the sides. Fill tin with hot stewed apple. Put
rest of mixture on to grease proof paper and then slip on top
of apple, pressing edges together. Bake in quick oven for 20
minutes. Serve hot with cream as pudding, or ice with lemon
icing and sprinkle with nuts and serve cold.

GERMAN COFFEE SLICE

2 or 3 apples
3 oz (85g) sugar
2 oz (57g) butter

1 egg
1/2 cup milk
8 oz (227g) S.R. flour

Beat butter and sugar to cream, add egg, milk and sifted flour. The mixture must be dry. Spread thinly over an oven tray which has been buttered, and sprinkle with dry breadcrumbs. Grate the peeled apples and spread over the top of the cake mixture.

TOPPING

3 oz (85g) sugar
3-1/2 oz (99g) plain flour

2-1/2 oz (71g) butter
1/2 teaspoon vanilla

Put all the dry ingredients into a bowl and work in the butter. Sprinkle evenly over the apple.
Place in a moderate oven (350 deg.) and cook for about 30-40 minutes until brown.

APPLE FRUIT CAKE

1 cup sugar
2 teaspoons mixed spice
1 lb (454g) mixed fruit
15 oz (426g) cooked drained apple

4 oz (113g) butter
1 teaspoon carb. soda

Put all the above ingredients into a saucepan and boil for 3 minutes. Allow to cool and then mix in 2 eggs (beaten) and 1 cup of self raising flour and 1 cup of plain flour sifted together. Line an 8 inch tin with paper. Pour cake mixture into the tin and bake for about 2 hours at 350 deg.F.

PLAIN APPLE CAKE

1 tablespoon water	3 apples
grated rind of 1 lemon	1/3 cup water

Peel, core and slice the apples and put into a saucepan with sugar, lemon rind and water. Cook until tender.

1 cup plain flour	2 eggs
3/4 cup cornflour	1/2 cup sugar
2 teaspoons baking powder	4 oz (113g) butter

Make cake by creaming the butter and sugar, add the eggs and then sifted flours and baking powder. Place half the mixture into a greased 7" x 10" tin, spread the pureed apple over it and cover with the remaining cake mixture. Bake in moderate oven 25-35 minutes. When cool, ice with lemon icing and sprinkle with cinnamon.

APPLE CAKE

4 oz (ll3g) sugar	1 egg
8 oz (227g) S.R. flour	a little milk
a little brown sugar for top	4 oz (113g) margarine
1/2 lb (225g) peeled apples (2 large sweet variety)	

Sieve flour, rub in margarine, add sugar and egg. Cut apple into neat, dice size pieces, add to cake mixture, mix well in and add a little milk to give a slow dropping consistency. Put into greased 7"- 8" cake tin. Bake one hour at 375-400 deg.F. Sprinkle with brown sugar after cooking. A little spice and currants can be added for extra flavour.

* * *

*Add a grated apple to your scone
dough for lovely moist scones.*

CHOCOLATE APPLE CAKE (NO EGGS)

4oz (115g) butter
1 lb (454g) apples
4 oz (115g) plain flour
1 level teaspoon carb. soda

1 cup (230g) sugar
1 teaspoon vanilla
2 tablespoons cocoa
1 cup S.R. flour

Cook apples with a little water until soft and mash finely. Sift flours and cocoa three times and return to sifter. Cream butter and sugar, add vanilla. Stir carb. soda all at once into hot apples and while still fizzing add to creamed butter and sugar. Beating well, add half the flour and beat again. Add remaining flour, stir well to mix. Pour into greased 8" square tin and bake 30-45 minutes in moderate oven.

CINNAMON APPLE CAKES

This easy one egg mixture makes two apple cakes with spicy topping.

1 egg
3 cups S.R. flour
2 cooking apples
1 teaspoon cinnamon

1 cup sugar
2oz (55g) butter
1-1/4 cups (275ml) milk
2 tablespoons brown sugar

Sift flour into a bowl, rub in butter until mixture resembles fine breadcrumbs. Add sugar. Beat in egg and milk until combined. Make a well in centre of dry ingredients, add milk mixture, mix well. Pour into two greased deep 7" cake tins.
Peel, quarter and core apples, slice thinly. Arrange apple slices neatly over the two cakes. Sprinkle over combined brown sugar and cinnamon. Bake in moderate oven for 35-40 minutes.

SLICED APPLE SHORT CAKE

1/2 cup sugar
1/2 cup sultanas
1 teaspoon cinnamon
grated rind of 1 lemon
2 cups sweetened cooked apple

1 egg
vanilla
2 cups S.R. flour
4 oz (113g) butter
1/2 teaspoon mixed spice

Cream butter and sugar, add vanilla and eggs and beat. Mix to firm dough with flour, halve the dough, roll out and place in 8" tin, drain apples, add rind, sultanas and spice. Cover first dough in tin, then roll second dough and cover apple. Bake 45 minutes at 350 deg.

APPLE CAKE

1/2 cup milk
1/2 cup sugar
2 cups S.R. flour

1 egg
1-1/2 tablespoons butter

Mix well, roll out, not too thick. On one half spread cold stewed apples, cover and bake in good hot oven.

UPSIDE DOWN APPLE CAKE

1 egg
1 cup S.R. flour
2oz (55g) butter

pinch salt
a little milk
1 tablespoon sugar

Rub flour, butter, sugar together, beat egg and add enough milk to make a soft dough. Roll out and place larger piece in a greased tin. Half fill with dry stewed apples and place smaller piece of dough on top. Join to the edges of other piece. Bake for 10-15 minutes in 500 deg. oven. Tip out onto plate, coat with butter then sprinkle with sugar and cinnamon mixture.

APPLE FRUIT CAKE

1 teaspoon ginger
1 cup sugar
1/2 lb (230g) margarine
2 teaspoons carb. soda
2-1/2 cups stewed unsweetened apples

1 teaspoon allspice
1 teaspoon cinnamon
1 lb (454g) mixed fruit
3-1/2 cups plain flour

Melt butter, sugar and soda in hot apple. Add sifted dry ingredients and fruit and mix well. Bake in large dish in moderate oven for 1-1/2 hours.

LORETTA'S APPLE CAKE

2oz (55g) sugar
2oz (55g) cornflour
1 teaspoon cinnamon
1 lb (454g) stewed apple (drained)

1 egg
1 tablespoon milk
4oz (113g) margarine
6oz (180g) S.R. flour

Sift flour, rub in butter, add sugar. Mix to a firm dough with beaten egg and milk. Knead well, divide in half. Line tin with half mixture and spread with apple, sprinkle with cinnamon and cover with rest of pastry. Bake in moderate oven 40-45 minutes. Ice with lemon icing.

APPLE CREAM SLICE

1 cup S.R. flour
stewed apple
4 oz butter
1 teaspoon each of cinnamon, ginger and mixed spice

1 egg
3oz sugar

Cream butter and sugar, add egg and beat. Sift spices with flour, add to creamed mixture. Spread half mixture into 8" greased tin, spread with cold apple. Place the remainder mixture on top. Bake 25 minutes at 350 deg. When cold, cover with whipped cream and sprinkle with cinnamon.

CARAMEL APPLE RING

1/2 teaspoon salt
2 tablespoons butter
1 tablespoon butter
8oz (227g) S.R. flour
1 dessertspoon sugar
extra 2 tablespoons brown sugar

3/4 cup milk
1/2 teaspoon cinnamon
1-1/2 cups cooked apples
1/2 teaspoon grated lemon rind
4 tablespoons brown sugar

Cream butter and brown sugar, spread over base and sides of 8" ring tin. Sift flour, salt and sugar into basin and rub in butter. Mix to soft dough with milk. Roll to oblong shape 1/4" thick. Spread with apple pulp mixed with extra brown sugar, lemon rind and cinnamon. Roll up to 2" thick. Cut into 2" slices. Place cut side down in ring tin. Bake 25 minutes in hot oven.

APPLE CAKE

3oz (85g) sugar
8oz (227g) flour
2oz (55g) butter
2 teaspoons baking powder

cinnamon
1 lb apples
2 tablespoons milk

Sift flour with baking powder, rub in butter, mix in 55g of sugar, add enough milk to make a stiff paste, roll out 1/4" thick, lay on swiss roll tin. Peel and slice apples, arrange on top of pastry, sprinkle with sugar and cinnamon. Bake in hot oven for 25 minutes.

EGGLESS APPLE CAKE

2 teaspoons cinnamon
4oz (113g) margarine
extra 1-1/2 teaspoons cinnamon

2 cups S.R. flour
1 cup brown sugar
1/2 teaspoon nutmeg

1-1/2 cups cooked warm apple, into which put 2 teaspoons carb. soda

Cream butter & sugar, add apples etc., flour, 1 cup of walnuts may be added. Bake in moderate oven 1-1/2 hours. Ice and sprinkle with cinnamon.

31

APPLE CHEESE LOAF

4oz (113g) butter or marg.

1/2 teaspoon soda	2 eggs
1/2 teaspoon ground ginger	1-3/4 cups flour
1 teaspoon baking powder	3/4 cup sugar
1 cup grated unpeeled red apples	1/3 cup chopped
cup grated tasty cheese (cheddar)	walnuts

Beat together butter and sugar until creamy, add eggs one at a time, beating as you add. Sift together the dry ingredients, stir in about 1/3, then stir in grated apples, cheese and walnuts. When combined, mix in remainder of flour. Turn into a greased loaf tin (9" x 5") and bake in moderate oven about 1 hour, or until done when tested.

APPLE FRUIT CAKE

1 cup sugar	1/2 cup warm milk
1 cup S.R. flour	1 cup currants
1 cup plain flour	1 tablespoon butter
1 cup chopped raisins	1 teaspoon carb. soda
1 teaspoon mixed spice	1 cup cold stewed apple

Mix together the flours, sugar, chopped fruits and spice. Stir in well drained apple. Dissolve carb. soda in warm milk in which butter has been melted. Add fruit mixture, stir until well mixed. Turn into greased and paper lined 8" square cake tin. Bake in moderate oven for about 1-1/2 hours.

APPLE CAKE WITH CRUMBLE TOP

1 egg
1/2 cup sugar
2 cups S.R. flour

1/2 cup milk
stewed apples
1-1/2 tablespoons butter

Cream butter and sugar, add beaten egg and milk. Add flour
and form a stiff dough. Divide into 2 parts. Roll very thinly.
Place half into tin and cover with stewed apple (rather dry).
Sprinkle with cinnamon and cover with second half of mixture.

TOPPING

Mix together 1 cup S.R. flour, 1/2 cup sugar, 1/2 cup butter.
Rub together to form crumble. Spread evenly on top.
Bake in moderate oven for 20-30 minutes.

BOILED APPLE FRUIT CAKE

1 cup water
2 grated apples
1 cup brown sugar
8oz (227g) raisins
8oz (227g) sultanas
6oz (170g) butter

2 eggs
1 cup S.R. flour
2 tablespoons jam
1-1/4 cups plain flour
1 teaspoon carb. soda
1 teaspoon mixed spice

Put butter, sugar, sultanas, raisins, apples, water, spice and
jam into a large saucepan and simmer 5 minutes. Add soda
while hot and allow to cool. Stir in sifted flours and add lightly
beaten eggs. Bake in moderate oven for 1-1/4 hours.

APPLE TEA CAKE

1 egg
pinch salt
1/4 cup sugar
1 dessertspoon butter

1 apple
1 cup S.R. flour
a little milk to mix

Sift flour and salt, add sugar and rub in fat. Mix to a cake-like batter with beaten egg and a little milk. Turn mixture into greased sandwich tin and arrange a thinly sliced apple on top, half in and half out of mixture. Sprinkle with cinnamon and one dessertspoon of sugar. Bake in moderate oven (moderate to hot) for about 25 minutes. Serve hot or cold, plain or buttered.

EGGLESS APPLE CAKE

teaspoon cinnamon
4oz (113g) sugar
4oz (113g) margarine

2 cups S.R. flour
1/2 teaspoon mixed spice
1 cup apple pulp (stewed)

Cream butter and sugar, add sifted flour and spices then add stewed apple and bake in moderate oven.

DANISH APPLE CAKE

1 cup S.R. flour
4oz (113g) butter
cup castor sugar
1 large egg lightly beaten
2 apples, peeled and sliced

1/2 teaspoon cinnamon
2 tablespoons sultanas
1 teaspoon brown sugar
2 teaspoons lemon juice
1/2 teaspoon powdered ginger

sweetened whipped cream for serving
1 tablespoon chopped walnuts (optional)

Line the bottom of an 8" greased sandwich tin with greased paper, beat butter and sugar to a cream, add egg then sifted flour and salt. Spread half in tin. Cover with apples, sprinkle with cinnamon, ginger, brown sugar, lemon juice and sultanas, then with rest of mixture. Add walnuts. Bake at 350 deg.F for 45 minutes. Serve with cream. Serves 8.

APPLE & BANANA SHORTCAKE

1 egg	1 passionfruit
1 banana	1/4 teaspoon salt
4oz (113g) butter	1 cup plain flour
1/2 cup castor sugar	1 cup S.R. flour
2 grated apples	grated rind & juice 1/2 lemon

Cream butter and sugar lightly add egg. Mix in flours, sifted, and salt. Divide in two. Roll into 2 rounds. Put one in base of greased 8" cake tin (round). Cover with grated apple, sliced bananas and passionfruit. Sprinkle with grated rind and juice of 1/2 lemon. Add 1 tablespoon sugar, cover with dough, brush with water, sprinkle castor sugar. Bake in moderate oven 35-40 minutes.

APPLE FILLING FOR CAKE OR TART

2 large apples	1/2 cup sugar	rind of 1 lemon

Grate apples into saucepan, add lemon rind and sugar. Cook 5 minutes, stirring constantly. When cold, spread on to cake.

APPLE CAKE

1 egg	2 apples
1/2 cup sugar	cinnamon
4oz (113g) butter	1/3 cup milk
2 cups S.R. flour	

Sift flour, add sugar. Rub in butter until mixture resembles fine breadcrumbs. Peel apples, cut into small pieces, fold into flour mixture. Add beaten egg and milk. Mix well. Spoon mixture into greased and paper lined 8" ring tin. Bake in moderate oven 45-50 minutes. Remove from oven, sprinkle top with cinnamon. Allow to cool a little before turning out of tin. Serve warm as dessert with custard, or serve as a cake. Serves 4 - 6.

EGGLESS SANDWICH WITH APPLE

2oz (55g) butter   1 cup sugar
l-1/2 cups S.R. flour   1 cup warm stewed apple
1 teaspoon carb. soda 2 dessertspoons dark cocoa
1/2 teaspoon nutmeg & cinnamon

Beat butter & sugar together and add soda mixed with apple. Add spices and cocoa mixed with flour. Bake in sandwich tins for 20-30 minutes. When cold, fill and ice with favourites such as whipped cream and chocolate icing.

SPICED APPLE CAKE

about 1/2 pint milk 3oz (85g) butter
2oz (55g) sugar   1 lb (454g) stewed apples
5oz (140g) flour   1 level dessertspoon baking powder
2 teaspoons cinnamon 3oz (85g) cornflour

Put dry ingredients into a basin. Rub butter in with enough milk to make a stiff paste. Cut in half, roll each out to fit a sandwich tin. Put apple between and bake 1/2 hour gas 375 deg., electric 425 deg.

APPLE NUT CAKE

1 cup sifted plain flour   1 egg, well beaten
1 teaspoon baking soda 1/4 teaspoon salt
1 cup brown sugar   3/4 teaspoon cinnamon
1/4 cup shortening   2 teaspoons lemon juice
2 cups chopped raw apple 1 cup chopped nuts

Sift together flour, soda, salt & cinnamon. Place shortening in a bowl and add sugar gradually, beating until fluffy. Add egg gradually, beating well. Stir in apples & lemon juice. Add dry ingredients in three portions, beating only enough to blend. Next, beat only until smooth; blend in chopped nuts. Lightly grease 8"x8"x2" tin before pouring in. Bake at 350 deg. for about 45 minutes.

QUICK APPLE CAKE

1/4 teaspoon salt
1/2 cup chopped nuts
2 cups chopped apple
1 teaspoon cinnamon

1 egg
1 cup sugar
1/2 cup margarine
1 cup S.R. flour

Mix all ingredients together until smooth. Bake in 9" square pan 35 minutes at 350 degrees.

QUICK APPLE SPONGE

May be eaten as a cake or dessert.

Take an unfilled plain sponge and cut through the centre. Spread with apricot or raspberry jam. Spread with drained stewed apple. Place other half on top and cover with whipped cream.

APPLE SLICE CAKE

2 cups drained, stewed apple
2 tablespoons apricot jam
2oz (57g) butter
1 packet plain cake mix

1 egg
1/4 cup coconut
1 cup water

Divide cake mix in two. Add coconut to one half, and rub in butter. Press into well greased 7" x 11" lamington tin. Bake in moderate oven 10 minutes. Heat stewed apple in saucepan and fold in apricot jam. Add water and egg to other half of mixture and beat well.
Spread hot apple over hot base and cover with cake mixture. Bake in moderate oven 20-25 minutes or until golden brown. Dust with icing sugar and cut into slices. Serve hot with ice cream, or cold with sweetened whipped cream.

SPICED APPLE CHEESE CAKE

6oz (170g) butter
1/3 cup sugar
1 egg yolk

1 dessertspoon water
grated rind 1 lemon
2 cups plain flour

CHEESE FILLING

8oz (227g) cream cheese
1/3 cup sugar

2 eggs
1 teaspoon vanilla

APPLE FILLING

4 large apples
1/2 cup raisins
1/4 cup rum

1 teaspoon cinnamon
1 tablespoon sugar

PASTRY: Cream butter and sugar, add egg yolk, water and rind. Work in sifted flour to form soft dough. Press out flat, chill for 1 hour. Roll out 3/4 of chilled pastry, line 8" springform pan. Freeze rest of pastry. Spread half cream cheese mixture over base of pastry, spoon in apple filling, pour over rest of cheese mixture. Press mixture down firmly; grate remaining frozen pastry over top. Bake in moderately slow oven for 2 hours.

CHEESE FILLING: Beat cheese until soft, add sugar, beat until light and fluffy. Add eggs and vanilla. Beat until smooth.

APPLE FILLING: Peel and core apples, slice thinly. Mix with the remaining apple filling ingredients.

LITTLE APPLE CAKES

2 cups stewed apples
3 cups S.R. flour
8oz (227g) butter

1 cup sugar
2 eggs
a little milk

Sift flour, add sugar and rub in butter. Beat eggs well, add milk and pour on to dry ingredients and knead together. Cut into rounds and line greased patty tins, put a spoonful of stewed apple on each and cover with another round of pastry after having moistened the edge of lower round with water to make the two rounds adhere. Bake in moderate oven 10-20 minutes. Sprinkle with icing sugar when cold.

APPLE SAUCE CAKE

2 cups S.R.flour
1/2 teaspoon carb. soda
1/2 teaspoon cinnamon
1/2 teaspoon nutmeg
1/4 teaspoon ground cloves
1 cup unsweetened stewed apple

4oz (ll3g) shortening
1 cup sugar
2 eggs
1/2 cup walnuts
3/4 cup dates

First stew apples and cool. Beat butter and sugar together, add eggs, then sift in flour and spices, and carb. soda. Add Apples, well drained, dates and walnuts. Place in a greased 8" square tin and bake 35 minutes at 400 deg. F. When cold, ice with lemon icing and sprinkle with cinnamon.

APPLE NUT LOAF

6oz (170g) sugar
1-1/2 tablespoons sour milk
1 large cooking apple
2 teaspoons grated lemon rind
2oz (57g) chopped walnuts
1 teaspoon baking powder

1 teaspoon carb. soda
4oz (113g) butter
2 eggs
8oz (227g) flour
pinch salt

Dissolve soda in milk. Sieve flour and baking powder and salt. Cream the butter and sugar until light and fluffy, add the whisked eggs, beating well as you add. Stir in flour, milk, nuts and lemon rind. Add the peeled and finely chopped apple and mix well. Turn into greased loaf tin and bake about 45 minutes in moderate oven. When cold, ice with lemon icing. Nice eaten as it is, or after a day or so can be buttered.

CHOCOLATE UPSIDE DOWN CAKE

APPLE MIXTURE

3oz (85g) butter

3oz (85g) light brown sugar

2 cups stewed apple

2 tablespoons sugar

Cream butter and brown sugar and spread over sides and bottom of an 8" cake tin. Mix the sugar with the apples and place into tin.

CAKE MIXTURE

2oz (57g) butter

1/4 cup milk

1 teaspoon vanilla

4oz (113g) castor sugar

5oz (141g) S.R. flour

1 tablespoon cocoa

pinch salt

1 egg

Cream butter and sugar, beat in the egg, add sifted dry ingredients alternately with the milk and vanilla. Spread over the apples in tin. Bake at 350 deg. for 3/4 - 1 hour. Leave in tin 5 minutes before turning on to wire rack. When cold, top with whipped chocolate cream and sprinkle with grated chocolate. Decorate with sliced raw apple.

CHOCOLATE CREAM

1 tablespoon icing sugar & 1 teaspoon cocoa, mix together and add to 1/2 pint cream. Whip until thick and pile on to apple cake. Serve hot as a dessert with chocolate sauce by adding 1 tablespoon cocoa and an extra tablespoon sugar to one pint of your favourite custard sauce recipe.

APPLE & GINGER DELIGHT

5 large cooking apples

8oz (227g) ginger nuts

whipped cream & cherries

sugar

water

green colouring

Stew apples with sugar and water. Cool and colour pale green. Crush ginger nuts finely. Place a layer of apple in bottom of parfait glasses, then alternate layers of ginger nuts. Swirl with cream and decorate with cherry or after dinner mint.

DANISH APPLE CAKE (NO BAKING)

2 lb cooking apples, peeled, cored & sliced
4 tablespoons water
10oz(283g) fresh breadcrumbs
1oz (28g) grated chocolate
1/4 pint cream

6oz(170g) butter
1oz(28g) castor sugar
1/2 teaspoon vanilla

Put prepared apples into pan with the water and cook over low heat with the pan covered, until apples are soft and pulpy. Stir in sugar and vanilla. Melt the butter in a frying pan, add the breadcrumbs and, stirring all the time, fry crumbs until they have absorbed all the butter and are golden brown. Sprinkle a third of the crumbs over the base of a dish, then cover them with half the apples and repeat the layers ending with the crumbs. Leave in a cool place overnight. Next day, whisk the cream until it holds its shape, then spoon it around the edge of each dessert and scatter with grated chocolate.

APPLE PARFAIT

5 large cooking apples
a little water
lemon rind
2 cloves
honey

10 ginger nut biscuits
2-1/2 cups thick vanilla
custard (cooled)
vanilla icecream
glace cherries

Peel, core and slice the apples. Cook with lemon rind and cloves in a very little water until soft. Sweeten with honey to taste. Allow to cool, remove the cloves and lemon rind. In parfait glasses put layers of apple, crushed ginger nuts and custard. When ready to serve add scoop of icecream and a glace cherry.

APPLE MOUSSE

2-1/2 lb (1-1/2kg) cooking apples (Granny Smiths are best)
1/2oz (14g) gelatine dissolved in 1/4 cup water
2oz (57g) butter   3 tablespoons honey
1/2 pint cream   grated rind of 1/2 lemon

Peel, core and slice apples finely and cook slowly in butter
until they are pulpy, then add the lemon rind and beat until
the apples become a puree. Add the honey and dissolved
gelatine and set aside to cool. Whip the cream lightly, and
carefully fold into the apple mixture. Turn into a greased
mould and leave aside to set.

APPLE SNOW

4 large cooking apples   4 tablespoons sugar
piece of lemon rind   little water
2 egg whites   1 teaspoon lemon juice

Peel, core and slice apples. Put into saucepan with lemon
rind and juice, sugar and 3 tablespoons water. Cook gently
until the apples are tender. Remove lemon rind then mash
apples to a pulp. Cool. Beat egg whites until soft peaks form,
gradually beat in apple pulp. Serve in small dessert glasses,
top with a spoonful of whipped cream.

Make boiled custard with yolks of eggs and serve with apple
snow instead of cream.

Add 1/2 teaspoon cinnamon to make cinnamon snow.

APPLE ICE CREAM

4 good sized cooking apples
1/2 teaspoon orange rind
juice of 1/2 orange
sugar to taste
1/2 pint cream

3 tablespoons sherry
4 tablespoons apricot jam
juice of 1/2 lemon
1 tablespoon red currant jelly

Peel apples and gently cook in covered pan with half the lemon juice. When cooked, sweeten to taste and mash to puree, then add rest of lemon juice, rind and juice of the orange, apricot jam and sherry. Mix well and chill. Whip the cream (reserve a little for decoration) and add to the puree. Mix and freeze but on no account freeze too hard, it must be softish. Serve in glasses, decorate with a spot of cream and a dab of redcurrant jelly.

APPLE PYRAMID

1 round layer of white cake
1-1/2 cups whipped cream
1/2 teaspoon vanilla

2 cups thick cold apple sauce
1/4 cup slivered almonds
2 cups lemon custard

Place cake on platter, cover with custard and allow to set for a few minutes. Add chilled apple sauce to form pyramid in centre. Whip cream with sugar and vanilla and pile over cake. Sprinkle with almonds. Chill 30 minutes before serving.

CUSTARD FILLING:
Put 2 cups of milk into a saucepan with 1/4 cup of sugar and bring to boil. Mix 3 egg yolks, 3 tablespoons cornflour, vanilla essence and enough milk to make a smooth paste. Stir into milk when just at boil and stir to required thickness. Stir in 2 teaspoons grated lemon rind.

AUTUMN PUDDING

1 lb (454g) cooking apples   8oz (227g) sugar
1 lb (454g) blackberries   8 slices stale bread

Peel, core and slice apples and put them in a pan with the blackberries, add water and stew the fruits over a low heat for about 15 minutes, until all are tender. Stir in sugar and slightly mash the fruit. Cut crusts from bread, then line the base and sides of a buttered small to medium deep casserole dish with some of the slices. Pour in one third of the fruit mixture, cover this with more bread and repeat the layers ending with the bread on top.
Put a plate on top of mixture and a weight on top of that. Leave it like this overnight. To serve, remove weight on plate, loosen pudding around edges and turn it out onto a serving plate. The bread should have absorbed all the juices, but the pudding should stand erect. Serve it cut into wedges with cream.

APPLE & RAISIN PANCAKES

PANCAKE MIXTURE

1 cup S.R. flour   1/2 cup sour milk or fresh
pinch of salt   with 1 teaspoon vinegar
2 tablespoons sugar   1 dessertspoon melted butter
1 egg   1/4 teaspoon carb. soda

Sift dry ingredients, add sugar, egg, milk and butter. Beat until smooth and thoroughly mixed. Stand 1/2 hour.

PANCAKE FILLING

Cook together stewed apple, raisins and cinnamon, and keep warm. Make pancakes in usual way and fill with apple and raisin mixture, serve with cream and/or icecream.

APPLE FRITTERS

2oz (57g) plain flour
pinch salt
1 dessertspoon melted butter
apples, peeled and cut into rings

1/2 cup warm water
white of one egg

Sift flour and salt. Make a well in the centre of the flour and pour in melted butter and warm water. Work until smooth and beat well. Allow to stand for at least 1/2 hour. Beat egg white until very stiff and fold into batter. Dip the slices of apple into the batter and deep fry in copha until golden brown. Drain, roll in sugar and serve hot with icecream.

APPLE CRUNCH

FILLING:
1 lb (454g) cooking apples, 4oz (II3g) sugar

TOPPING:
2 tablespoons butter
1 tablespoon golden syrup
2 cups cornflakes

Filling: Quarter, peel and thinly slice apples into a saucepan with the sugar and 1 tablespoon of water. Bring to boil, cover with lid and cook gently until tender. Turn into a 1-1/2 pint baking dish and set aside.

Topping: Melt butter and syrup over low heat in a saucepan, remove from heat and stir in cornflakes until thoroughly coated. Spoon over apples, spread evenly and bake in centre of moderate oven 350 degrees for 20 - 30 minutes. Topping should be crisp and golden brown. Serve warm with cream.

APPLE & DATE CRISP

2 cooking apples
1 cup dates
1/2 cup water
1 teaspoon grated lemon rind
1 cup rolled oats
sprinkling of lemon juice

1-1/2 cups S.R. flour
1/2 teaspoon cinnamon
6oz (125g) margarine
1/2 cup raw sugar
extra 2 tablespoons raw
sugar

Combine dates, water, lemon rind and sugar in a saucepan
and cook for 2-3 minutes until dates are soft, remove from
stove, add lemon juice, beat with wooden spoon until smooth.
Allow this mixture to cool. Sift flour and cinnamon. Rub in
margarine, add sugar and rolled oats. Grease 7-1/4 square tin
and line with paper.
Press 2/3 of mixture into tin, spread with date mixture. Peel,
core and thinly slice apples and place all over the date mixture, Place remaining oat mixture on top of apples and press
down well. Bake in moderate oven about 45 minutes. Serve
warm or cold with cream or icecream.

CARROT & APPLE PUDDING

1 cup S.R. flour
1 teaspoon baking powder
1/2 level teaspoon nutmeg
1/2 teaspoon cinnamon
1/2 teaspoon mixed spice
6 oz grated margarine
2 eggs

2 tablespoons treacle
1/2 cup sugar (brown)
1 cup grated carrot
1 cup grated apple
3/4 cup sultanas
1/2 cup soft bread crumbs

Sift flour, baking powder and spices together. Combine sugar,
treacle, carrot, apple, sultanas, breadcrumbs and margarine in
bowl. Beat eggs and add mixture, fold in sifted dry ingredients. Turn into well greased pudding basin, cover and steam
2-1/2 hours. Serve hot with icecream or vanilla custard.

QUICK APPLE STREUSEL

Grate 1 lb (454g) Granny Smith apples into pie plate and sprinkle with brown sugar and cinnamon. Sultanas may be added if desired.

STREUSEL TOPPING:
Rub together 3oz (85g) butter, 4oz (113g) sugar and 4 oz S.R. flour until mixture resembles fine bread crumbs. Sprinkle topping over apple and bake in oven at 350 degrees for approximately 15-20 minutes.

FRENCH APPLE TART

Baked 7" or 8" biscuit pastry case (packet pastry mix with 1 egg and a little sugar is good). Thicken hot stewed apple with egg yolk or custard powder and part fill cooked pastry case. Arrange sliced raw apple to cover stewed apple. Mix a little sieved apricot jam and hot water and glaze the raw apple with this. Bake in oven until edges are browned.

LAZYMAN'S APPLE PIE

4 cups sliced uncooked apple
teaspoon cinnamon
3/4 cup S.R. flour
1 cup sugar

1/2 cup warm water
3 oz (85g) butter
pinch salt

Place layers of apples in a pie dish, sprinkling each layer with sugar and a little cinnamon and warm water. Rub butter into sifted flour and salt. Place this crumbly mixture on top of fruit. Cover top of pie with aluminium foil and cook in moderate oven about 1-1/2 hours.

APPLE PUFFS

Boil to a syrup for 5 minutes: 1 cup sugar, 1 cup water and 1/2 teaspoon colouring.
Place in a greased pie dish, 12 large cooking apples finely sliced, and pour the syrup over. Mix together 1-1/2 cups S.R. flour, 1/2 cup margarine and 3/4 cup milk.
Drop teaspoonfulls on top of the apple, making a dent in each. Mix together 2 tablespoons butter and sugar and 1/2 teaspoon cinnamon, and place a small amount on each dent. Bake in moderate oven for 25-30 minutes.

NOVEL APPLE PUDDING

4 cooking apples
3/4 cup sugar
1 cup cold water

2 tablespoons S.R. flour
1 tablespoon butter
pinch salt

Peel and core apples, cut into quarters and arrange in dish. Rub butter into flour, add sugar and salt, then water. Mix lightly and pour mixture over apples. Bake for 35 minutes in moderately hot oven (220 degrees C). Serve with custard.

CRUNCHY APPLE & BANANA PUDDING

3 large apples
3 bananas

1/2 cup water
3 tablespoons sugar

Peel, core and slice apples into pie dish, slice bananas and add evenly over apples. Add water and sugar.

Mix: 1/2 cup S.R. flour, 1/2 cup sugar, 1/2 teaspoon vanilla, & 1 tablespoon butter to resemble fine breadcrumbs, and sprinkle over fruit. Bake in moderate oven until apple is tender and top is golden brown, 35-40 minutes. Delicious served hot or cold with cream, icecream or custard.

QUICK APPLE DESSERT

cinnamon   stewed apples
breadcrumbs   butter   sugar

Lightly butter a pie dish and sprinkle breadcrumbs on bottom
and sides. Add layer of apple, sprinkle with sugar & cinnamon,
add another layer of breadcrumbs, apple, etc., until dish is
full, ending with layer of breadcrumbs. Sprinkle top with sugar
and cinnamon and dot with butter. Bake in oven until nicely
browned. Serve hot with icecream.

FRUIT CURLS

1/2 cup cold water   1 tablespoon sugar
1-1/2 cups S.R. flour   1 teaspoon cinnamon
125g butter or marg.   1/2 cup sultanas or raisins
TOPPING: 2 tablespoons sugar, 1-2 tablespoons butter,
                 1-1/2 cups boiling water

Make a soft dough with flour, butter & water. Knead lightly
and roll out to approximately 12"x18". Cover dough with grated
apple & sultanas and sprinkle with sugar and cinnamon. Roll
up like jam roll and slice into 1/2" pieces. Place cut side down
in baking dish, then add topping by sprinkling with sugar, dot-
ting with butter and pouring boiling water over.
Bake in moderate oven about 30 minutes until golden brown.
Serve with cream or custard.

APPLE ROLY POLY

2 cups S.R. flour   3 apples
3 oz (90g) butter or marg.   1/3 cup sultanas
1/3 cup butter   3 tablespoons apricot jam
1 tablespoon sugar
 Sift flour, rub in butter, add water, mix to a firm dough, place
on lightly floured surface, knead lightly until smooth, roll to a
rectangular shape 25cm x 30cm. spread evenly with apricot

(continued on next page)

jam, peel apples, grate coarsely, spread over jam, sprinkle with sultanas. Roll up starting from long side, brush joins with water. Place joined side down on greased oven tray, brush top with water, sprinkle with sugar. Bake in moderate oven 30 to 35 minutes or until golden brown. Serve with cream or custard.

RICE & APPLE CUSTARD

1 cup cooked rice	2 eggs
3 tablespoons sugar	I-1/2 cups milk
2 large cooking apples	1 tablespoon butter

Put the cooked rice on bottom of an ovenproof dish. Peel, core and slice the apples on top of rice. Sprinkle with sugar and put small dabs of butter over apples. Add the milk and beaten eggs and pour over apples. Bake in moderate oven 350 degrees until custard is set. Allow to cool. Serve with cream.

APPLE & RICE MERINGUE

a few cloves	2 oz (57g) rice
1 oz (28g) butter	1 oz (28g) sugar
1-1/2 lbs (680g) apples	2 oz (57g) sugar
1/4 pt (156 mls) water	1/2 pt (315 mls) milk
thin strip lemon peel	1/4 pt (156 mls) water
whites 2 eggs and 2 tablespoons sugar for meringue	

Wash rice and put in a saucepan with the water, cook gently until all water is absorbed. Add milk and simmer gently until absorbed, then add 1 oz sugar. Peel, core and cut up apples rather thickly and put on to stew with water, butter, cloves, lemon rind and 2 oz sugar. Cook until tender. Remove cloves and lemon peel and mash apples well with fork. Spread rice over. Make meringue and pile on top of rice, put in cool oven until meringue is set.

APPLE DUMPLINGS

Quantity of short crust pastry and required number of large apple halves, peeled and cored. Roll out pastry thinly. Cut a square slightly larger than the apple half and wrap up each piece in the pastry. Place in baking dish, joined side down, pour milk over until apple parcels are about half covered, sprinkle with sugar generously and bake in moderate oven until pastry is golden brown and apples are tender. When cooked there is a creamy sauce at the bottom of the dish.

DUTCH APPLE PIE

1 egg
1/2 cup sugar
3 apples peeled & diced
1 teaspoon baking powder
3 tablespoons flour

1 teaspoon cinnamon
1/4 teaspoon nutmeg
1/4 teaspoon salt
1 tablespoon butter
1/2 cup chopped walnuts

Beat eggs and sugar until frothy. Combine apples with flour, baking powder, cinnamon, nutmeg, salt and walnuts; blend well and stir in beaten eggs. Turn into buttered pie dish and dot with butter. Bake 325 degrees for 30 minutes.

APPLE TOPPING
A change from pastry

2 cups fine breadcrumbs
   (fresh)
3/4 cup sugar

1 cup coconut
1 egg (well beaten)
grated rind of 1 lemon

Mix and spread on top of stewed apples and bake until golden brown. Serve with cream.

STEAMED APPLE PUDDING

3 apples
pinch salt
2 cups S.R. flour

1 teaspoon sugar
1 tablespoon butter or good
    dripping

Rub butter into flour and salt. Add sugar, mix into soft dough with equal parts of milk and water. Grease pudding basin with butter and slice one apple on bottom, cover with dough 1" thick, then slice 2 apples onto dough, sprinkle with sugar and 1 tablespoon water, then put rest of dough on top. Cover and steam for 1-1/2 hours.

APPLE SPONGE

Half fill a large casserole dish with hot stewed apples. Pour sponge mixture on top and bake 400 degrees approximately 25 minutes.
SPONGE TOP: 2 eggs, 1/2 cup sugar, 1/3 cup S.R. flour and 1 tablespoon cornflour. Beat eggs until thick and frothy, then gradually add sugar. Fold in sifted flour.

IRISH APPLE CAKE

250g flour
125g sugar
3 or 4 cooking apples
1/2 cup milk

1 rounded teaspoon baking pdr.
125g butter
1 egg (beaten)

Mix together flour, baking powder and sugar. Chop butter coarsely and add (do not cream or rub it in). Slice the peeled, cored apples in and then stir in the beaten egg and milk to make a fairly stiff batter (this will be quite lumpy with apples and butter, but this is correct). Pour into greased 8" sandwich tin and bake for about an hour, in a moderate oven. Serve hot with custard sauce or cream.

BAKED APPLE DESSERT (SELF-SAUCING)

1 tablespoon castor sugar
1 cup brown sugar
1 cup S.R. flour
pinch salt
cinnamon

2 cups boiling water
1 cup chopped apples
2 tablespoons butter
1 tablespoon lemon juice
1/2 cup milk

Sift together flour and salt, add castor sugar. Then add apple and milk. Mix to a scone-like dough. Place in a large baking dish as the mixture bubbles up during cooking. Blend brown sugar, lemon juice, boiling water and butter (using the same basin the dough was mixed in). Pour over the mixture in the baking dish and sprinkle cinnamon. Bake about 25 minutes in moderate oven. When cooked this pudding has a golden biscuit topping and a tasty sauce beneath. Serve with stiffly whipped sweetened cream or icecream, but it is nice by itself.

APPLE DESSERT CAKE

1 cup cream
1 cup sugar (optional)
1 level teaspoon cinnamon
1 cup well drained cold stewed apple
TOPPING:
1 grated raw apple
3 teaspoons sugar

283g S.R. flour
pinch salt
3 eggs

1 teaspoon cinnamon

Beat together cream, sugar, salt until slightly thickened. Add the well beaten eggs, beating as you add. Lightly stir in the sifted flour and cinnamon. Then add the cold stewed apple mixing until smooth. Pour into a well greased and lined 9" square tin. Sprinkle with raw apple and combine cinnamon and sugar. Bake in moderate oven for 55-60 minutes. Serve warm or cold with whipped cream or icecream.

DELICIOUS APPLE AMBER

1-1/2 lb (680g) apples	rind and juice of 1 lemon
1/3 cup sugar	2 eggs separated
1-1/2 oz (42g) butter	extra 2 tablespoons sugar

Set oven temperature at 350 degrees. Peel, core and slice apples. In heavy saucepan, combine apples, sugar, butter and rind and juice of lemon. Cook until tender. With a fork or in a blender puree apple until smooth. Beat egg yolks into apple puree and pour into a large pie dish. Whisk egg white until very stiff, fold in extra sugar. Pile meringue over apples and sprinkle with a little sugar. Bake in bottom of moderate oven for 15-20 minutes or until meringue is golden brown.

APPLE BREAD & BUTTER PUDDING

5 apples	2-1/2 cups milk
1/4 cup sugar	3 eggs
2 tablespoons water	1 tablespoon sugar (extra)
6 thin slices bread	1 tablespoon grated lemon rind
butter	1 cup sultanas

Peel, core and slice apples into saucepan with sugar and water and cook covered 5-10 minutes. Butter bread lightly, remove crusts and arrange slices in layers in greased oven-proof dish. Spread each layer generously with apple pulp and sprinkle with lemon rind and sultanas. Beat together eggs, milk and extra sugar. Pour over bread. Let stand 15 minutes, then sprinkle topping over. Bake in moderately slow oven 40 minutes. Serve with cream or custard.

TOPPING:

30g butter	3 tablespoons sugar
2 cup S.R. flour	2 tablespoons coconut

Sift flour, add coconut and sugar. Rub in butter until mixture resembles fine breadcrumbs.

APPLE GINGER PUDDING

2 apples
sugar and cinnamon
1-1/2 cups flour
1 teaspoon ground ginger
1 teaspoon mixed spice

1 cup warm milk
2 tablespoons golden syrup
2 tablespoons butter
1 teaspoon baking soda
pinch salt

Peel, core and slice apples into greased pudding basin and sprinkle with sugar and cinnamon. Sift dry ingredients together. Warm milk, golden syrup and butter and stir in soda. Add to sifted dry ingredients and blend. Pour this mixture over apples. Cover basin and steam for 2 hours.

APPLE COTTAGE PUDDING

3/4 cup sugar
2 eggs
1/2 cup flour
1-1/2 teaspoons baking powder
whipped cream or ice cream

1/2 teaspoon salt
1/2 cup chopped nuts
1 cup stewed apple
1 teaspoon vanilla

Beat sugar, egg thoroughly. Sift flour, baking powder, salt, and then blend into egg mixture. Add nuts, apple, vanilla, and mix well. Pour into 9" greased pie dish and bake in moderate oven 350 degrees, for 35-40 minutes. Serve warm or cold with whipped cream or ice cream. Serves 6-8.

AMERICAN APPLE DESSERT CAKE

2 cups sugar
4 oz (113g) margarine
2 eggs
4 cups diced apple

2 cups S.R. flour
1 teaspoon salt
1 teaspoon cinnamon
1/2 teaspoon nutmeg

Cream margarine, sugar, add eggs and beat well. Then add apples and dry ingredients. Bake in 9"X13" pan for about 1 hour in a moderate oven. Serve hot or cold with whipped cream or ice cream.

BAKED APPLE ROLL

1-1/2 cups flour
1 teaspoon cream of tartar
1/2 teaspoon carb. soda

2 tablespoons butter
pinch salt
a little milk

Rub well together and mix to a dough with milk then roll out
1/4" thick and spread with the following:

2 grated apples
3 tablespoons sultanas
a little candied peel

2 tablespoons sugar
grated nutmeg

Roll up like a swiss roll and pinch ends together. Place in pie
dish and pour over the following syrup:
1/2 cup butter, 1/2 cup sugar and 1 cup boiling water.
Bake until golden brown in moderate oven about 1 hour.

Spread roll with grated apple and sliced banana and
sprinkle with sugar.

APPLE PUFF PUDDING

4 large cooking apples
2 tablespoons sugar
1/4 cup milk
1 egg

2 tablespoons butter or margarine
1 cup S.R. flour
pinch salt

Peel, core and slice apples, cook in a little water until soft, with
sugar to taste. Blend together butter and sugar, add egg and
beat well. Add sifted flour with salt and milk. Put layer of batter
into greased pudding basin, cover with layer of cooled apples.
Repeat until all batter and apples are used, ending with layer
of batter. Cover basin and steam 12 hours.
Serve warm, with cream or ice cream.

APPLE COBBLER

1-1/2 lb (680g) green apples
6 oz (170g) breadcrumbs
1/2 teaspoon cinnamon
1/4 pt (155 ml) hot water

2 tablespoons golden syrup
sugar to taste
butter

Peel and slice apples and place into an ovenproof dish, alternately with breadcrumbs. Mix together the golden syrup, water & cinnamon, and pour this over the last layer of breadcrumbs. Sprinkle with sugar and dot with butter. Bake 35-40 minutes in moderate oven. Serve hot with custard or ice cream.

SNOWBALLS

3 oz (85g) mixed dried fruit
4 large or 6-8 small apples
3 oz (85g) castor sugar

1 oz (28g) soft brown sugar
3 egg whites
3 oz (85g) icing sugar

Mix fruit with sugar. Peel and core apples and fill centres with fruit and sugar. Place in greased casserole dish with lid, and bake in centre of oven for 25 minutes at 375 degrees.
MAKE MERINGUE:
Whisk egg whites, add sugar and beat until stiff. Fold in icing sugar. Remove apples from the oven and cover each with meringue. Return to a cooler oven and bake further 15-30 minutes. Spike each snowball with almond slivers.

FRIED APPLES

6 cooking apples
brown sugar

1/4 cup butter

Quarter and core apples, do not peel. Melt butter in frying pan. Place apples, skin side down, in pan. Sprinkle generously with sugar. Add a little water, cover and cook slowly until tender and candied. Serve hot with cream.

APPLE ROLY POLY

2 cups S.R. flour   1 large apple, grated
4 oz (113g) margarine   1 tablespoon sultanas
pinch salt   2 tablespoons chopped dried apricots

Rub margarine into flour and salt, add enough water to make stiff dough. Roll out thinly into a rectangle and sprinkle with grated apple, sultanas and dried fruit (any dried fruit is suitable). Roll up like a swiss roll and seal ends. Place into a large baking dish. Mix together 2 cups boiling water, 1/2 cup brown sugar and 2 tablespoons of butter, and pour this over. Bake in a moderate oven.

APPLE SPONGE PUDDING

Boil enough apples to half fill a medium size pie dish.
BATTER: Mix 1/2 cup sugar, 2 oz (55g) butter, add 1 egg and 1/2 cup milk. Sift in 1 cup S.R. flour. Pour over fruit which must be boiling. Cook 20 minutes at 375 degrees. This batter can be used over any fruit.

SPONGE TOP FOR STEWED APPLES

Beat together 1/3 cup sugar and 2 eggs until light and fluffy. Add 3/4 cup S.R. flour and pinch of salt with a little milk. Place on top of fruit and cook at 450 degrees for 15 minutes. Make sure fruit is boiling first.

APPLE & RAISIN SOUFFLE

3 cups stale breadcrumbs
4 medium cooking apples
3 eggs
pinch of salt

1/2 cup sugar
small cup raisins
2 tablespoons rum

Soak the breadcrumbs in milk. Pour the rum over the raisins. Peel, core and finely chop the apples. Drain the surplus milk from the breadcrumbs, then add the apples, sugar & raisins. Mix well. Add the egg yolks one at a time, stirring well, and a pinch of salt. Whisk egg whites and fold into mixture. Pack the mixture lightly into a deep well buttered dish standing in a pan of water. Cook in a 350 degree oven for about 45 minutes. Serve hot or cold with custard or cream.

APPLE & LEMON CRUNCH

SAUCE:

1/4 cup water
1-1/2 tablespoons flour
1 beaten egg

1 lemon rind & juice
pinch of salt

Put water, juice, rind, sugar and salt into saucepan, stir until smooth. Heat, and simmer 3 minutes. Remove from heat and add beaten egg.

CRUNCH:

1/2 cup brown sugar
1/2 cup coconut
3 oz (85g) melted butter
Mix all ingredients together.
2 apples, thinly sliced

3/4 cup flour
1 cup cornflakes

Place 1/3 of crunch mixture in ovenproof dish, cover with half the apples and half the lemon sauce. Repeat layers finishing with crunch mix. Bake uncovered at 350 degrees for approximately 25 minutes.

OSLO APPLE CAKE

CAKE MIXTURE:

1/2 lb S.R. flour

113g castor sugar

4 oz (113g) butter

1 egg

TOPPING:

3 large cooking apples

1 teaspoon grated lemon rind

57g sugar

1 tablespoon lemon juice

Place apples, sugar, lemon rind and juice in a saucepan and cook until tender, but firm. Rub butter into the flour until it resembles crumbs. Stir in castor sugar and then the beaten egg to form short pastry. Press 2/3 of pastry into a well greased 8" tin. Spread the cooled apple mixture evenly over the top. Roll out remaining pastry and cut into strips to form lattice work over the apple. Bake in moderate oven about 40 minutes.

APPLE CRUMBLE

Peel and slice apples and place in a greased casserole dish. Sprinkle with cloves, 3 tablespoons sugar and 3 tablespoons water.

STREUSEL TOPPING:

1 cup plain flour

3 tablespoons coconut

3 tablespoons brown sugar

Stir in 4 oz (113g) melted margarine. Place on top of apple and bake approximately 45 minutes at 400 degrees.

APPLE CUSTARD

1 egg
1/2 cup castor sugar
5 oz (141g) melted butter
6 apples, peeled and sliced thinly

1/4 cup sugar
1/2 teaspoon cinnamon
2 cups flour

Beat egg and sugar until thick. Add melted butter and sift in flour to form stiff dough. Press into 9" cake tin and arrange sliced apples in rows over cake. Sprinkle with sugar and cinnamon. Bake at 375 degrees for 1 hour.

CUSTARD

2 egg yolks
1/4 cup sugar

3/4 cup cream
vanilla essence

Beat egg yolks and sugar until smooth, stir in cream and vanilla. Pour this over the hot cake and return to oven for another 10 minutes or till custard is set.

APPLE HONEY CAKE

4 oz (113g) butter
1/2 cup honey
2 cups fresh breadcrumbs
2 tablespoons lemon juice

1 teaspoon cinnamon
4 cups stewed apple
1 tablespoon brown sugar

Mix butter and half the honey and breadcrumbs in pan. Mix well drained apple with the rest of honey and lemon juice. Put alternate layers of mixture in well greased dish, finishing with crumbs on top. Blend sugar and cinnamon, and sprinkle over top. Bake 30 minutes at 350 degrees.

SPICED APPLE & GINGER MERINGUE

2 eggs separated
2 tablespoons water
4 large cooking apples
1 teaspoon grated lemon rind
1/4 cup chopped preserved ginger

1/4 cup castor sugar
1/4 teaspoon ground cloves
2 tablespoons golden syrup

Peel and slice apples and cook slowly until tender with water and most of ginger, cloves, lemon rind and golden syrup. Beat yolks and add to apples in oven proof dish. Beat whites of eggs until stiff, add sugar and beat again. Cover apple mixture and sprinkle with remaining chopped ginger. Bake in oven 350 degrees for 15 minutes or until peaks are golden brown.

APPLE CUSTARD

Line a dish thickly with apples, cooked with as little water as possible, cover with a layer of breadcrumbs. Beat 2 egg yolks with 2 teaspoons sugar, add 1-1/2 cups milk, pour over apples and bake until set.

When cold, add a layer of lemon cheese, top with stiffly beaten egg whites and return to oven, cook until golden brown. Serve with cream.

BAKED APPLES

WITHOUT SKIN

Allow one large apple per person. Peel, core and leave whole.
Roll each in softened butter then in bread crumbs. Beat together a mixture of ground almonds, egg white and castor
sugar, and fill the cores liberally, letting the mixture come
over the top and spill down the sides. Bake in moderate oven
until the apples are cooked, usually about 45-60 minutes.
Serve with whipped cream or ice cream.

WITH SKIN

Allow one large apple per person. Wash and core and leave
whole, place in baking dish with a little water, then add any of
the following fillings:

1. Minced dried fruit (apricot, raisins, dates, prunes, and
   sultanas).
2. Whole dried apricots, prunes or dates.
3. Softened bread, chopped raisins or dates, chopped walnuts,
   cinnamon, brown sugar. Mix together and press into cores.
   Drizzle honey over each apple and bake until tender.
4. Mix together cinnamon and 1 tablespoon brown sugar.
   Sprinkle over top, in core, and dot with butter, drizzle honey
   or golden syrup, bake until tender.

FRENCH APPLE PUDDING

pinch salt   1/4 cup water
juice 1/2 lemon   1-1/2 cups S.R. flour
rind of 1 lemon   1/2 cup apricot jam
1/2 cup castor sugar   1 tablespoon brandy
2 oz (57g) butter   3 tablespoons powdered milk
2 cups coarsely chopped apples

Heat jam, brandy and lemon juice until it begins to boil. Cook
over low heat for 2 minutes. Cool slightly before pouring into
well greased pudding basin. Cream butter, sugar and lemon
rind until light and fluffy. Add egg and beat well, gradually add

water. Sift together flour, salt and powdered milk. Fold through creamed mixture. Finally add apple and mix well. Spoon over apricot mixture; cover with greased paper and steam 1-1/2 hours.

ROSY APPLES

1 orange	6 apples
1 cup water	1/2 cup white sugar
red food colouring	2 tablespoons brown sugar
2 oz (57g) chopped raisins	1 oz (28g) chopped walnuts

Wash apples and remove cores. Slit apple skins to prevent splitting while baking. Combine raisins, walnuts and brown sugar, and fill into apple cavities. Mix white sugar, water and enough food colouring to colour pink in saucepan. Stir over low heat until sugar has dissolved. Place stuffed apples in a greased oven proof dish, pour in prepared syrup. Cut oranges into thick slices and add. Bake in moderate oven 1 hour, basting occasionally.

APPLE MARMALADE

2 lemons	2 oranges
12 cups water	4 granny smith apples
6 lbs sugar	

Cut oranges and lemons finely and soak in water for 24 hours. Peel apples and cut thinly, add to above and boil 1 hour or until set.

APPLE JAM

6 apples	2 lemons
3/4 lb sugar to each pound of fruit	

Chop up apples, cover with water, boil 3/4 hour, then add sugar, then lemons. Boil gently for 2 hours.

APPLE & ORANGE JAM

1 lemon   3 large navel oranges
6 lbs sugar
3 large granny smith apples (no other kind will do)

Slice oranges and lemon thinly and cover with 12 cups water, let soak 24 hours. Cut apples into thin slices and boil all one hour. Add sugar and boil until it jells.
If the apple skins are boiled in a little water and the juice added, this helps to jell the fruit.

APPLE JELLY (JAM)

Wash, halve and quarter (including skins and seeds) sufficient apples to fill stockpot, cover with water. Boil until apples are soft, but not too pulpy. Strain through cheese cloth. Use an inverted stool, tying the cheese cloth to the legs, place a large bowl underneath to collect the strained liquid. All to stand for several hours dripping (do not squeeze). To make jelly, allow one cup of sugar to every cup of apple syrup. Boil gently until deep pink in colour, adding one tablespoon of strained lemon juice to every six cups of syrup about ten minutes before taking off fire. Skim off froth and bottle quickly. Use any apples early in season (straight off trees) or granny smiths later in the year provided they are fresh out of cold store.

APPLE JAM

To 5 lbs peeled and cored apples, add 2 cups of water and stew to a pulp. Add 4 lbs of sugar and 2 oz (57g) preserved ginger (cut fine). Boil until pinkish colour and ginger cooked. Use own discretion as to time.

APPLE CHUTNEY

2 teaspoons salt
2 cups malt vinegar
1/4 teaspoon cayenne pepper
1/2 cup firmly packed brown
        sugar

2 lbs apples
1 lb onions
8 oz raisins
2 teaspoons ground ginger
2 teaspoons crushed mustard seeds.

Peel, core and slice apples. Place in saucepan, add chopped raisins, sugar, finely chopped onions, ginger, mustard seeds, cayenne pepper and salt. Pour in vinegar and allow mixture to heat slowly, simmer for 1-2 hours until chutney is rich brown colour. Pour into small sterilised jars. When cold, cover to make air tight.

APPLE CHUTNEY

8 oz onions
3 lbs apples
4 oz currants
1 lb tomatoes
1 lb seeded raisins.
2-1/2 lbs brown sugar

1 teaspoon cloves
1-1/2 pints vinegar
1 oz preserved ginger
salt and cayenne pepper
1 dessertspoon made mustard

Peel and core apples. Stew gently in very little water until tender. Chop raisins and onions and peeled tomatoes. Put all ingredients in pan and simmer gently for 1-1/2 hours. Place in sterilised jars and cover.

TOFFEE APPLES

1 cup water
3 cups sugar
1 dessertspoon vinegar

wooden skewers
small red apples
red food colouring

Wash apples well. Dry, then remove stems and pierce apples with wooden skewers, refrigerate. Place sugar, water and vinegar in saucepan. Bring slowly to boiling point, stirring until all sugar is dissolved. Do not stir once mixture has reached boiling point. Boil steadily until toffee turns a deep straw colour and forms a hard ball when tested in cold water. Colour red with food colouring. Dip apples into toffee, swirl around to coat them, stand upright on waxed paper to set.

MUESLI

1/2 lemon
1 tablespoon dried fruit
1 tablespoon wheat germ
1/2 cup rolled or instant oats

3 teaspoons honey
2 teaspoons chopped nuts
1 apple
milk

Mix together the oatmeal and wheat germ and place into a breakfast bowl. Core and chop the apple, sprinkle with lemon juice. Add to cereal with chopped nuts and dried fruit. Sprinkle with honey and serve with milk.

SIMPLE APPLE MUESLI

1 tablespoon lemon juice
1 large apple (washed and
peeled)
2 cups milk

2 tablespoons honey
1 tablespoon sultanas
2 tablespoons rolled oats

Mix lemon juice, honey and milk together and pour over oats. Grate the apple into the mixture, stirring occasionally to prevent browning. Top with grated nuts and sultanas. Serve at once.

VARIATION
Other soft, fresh fruits may be added such as strawberries or bananas. Try yoghurt in place of milk.

APPLE CIDER

Cut as many apples as you like with peel and core, the more the bigger the quantity. Put into bowl or containers, cover with boiling water and let stand in a warm place for three days, then strain. To every 5 cups of liquid, add one cup of sugar then let stand for another 3 days, then strain. Bottle and seal or cork. Keep in warm place until ready.

APPLE CIDER

Slice enough apples to fill a 2 gallon bucket, unpeeled and uncored. Cover with 2 cups sugar, simmer a good handful of hops in one quart water and pour over apples. Then cover apples with boiling water.
Let stand 24 hours, strain and bottle, add a raisin to each bottle. Ready in seven days, sooner in hot weather.

CINNAMON APPLE SLICE

2 medium apples
8 oz butter
2 tablespoons golden syrup
2 cups S.R. flour
2 teaspoons cinnamon

1 cup raw sugar
2 cups coconut
1 cup sultanas
1 cup currants
2 eggs

Peel and grate apples into a large bowl, add sifted flour, cinnamon and sugar, add fruit. Melt butter, add golden syrup and add to other ingredients with lightly beaten eggs. Mix well and spread into tin. Bake 350 degrees for 1 hour. Ice with chocolate icing if desired.

BUTTERSCOTCH APPLE DUMPLINGS

2 apples
1 cup S.R. flour
2 teaspoons sugar

3 oz butter
pinch salt
2 tablespoons water

Sift flour, salt into bowl. Add sugar, rub in butter. Add water, mix to a soft dough. Extra water may be needed. Peel, core and quarter apples. Divide dough into 8 portions and carefully press each portion around apples.
Put in oven proof dish. Pour over sauce.

SAUCE
Combine all ingredients in saucepan: 1-1/2 oz butter, 1 cup brown sugar lightly packed, 1 tablespoon golden syrup, 1-1/2 cups water and bring to boil.
Bake uncovered in moderate oven 25-30 minutes.
Serve with ice cream and cream.

popular apples

RED DELICIOUS
Australia's most popular eating apple. Look for five prominent crowns around the base. The flesh is yellowish with a rich flavour, and acid content is low, so it is sweet to taste. Usually available March to January. This apple originated in the garden of Jesse Hiatt of Iowa, U.S.A. about 1880.

STURMER
Grown only in Tasmania, the Sturmer matures late March. Conical in shape with a distinct crown, it is greenish yellow in colour and acid to taste with a brisk flavour. It is mainly a cooking and processing apple, but because of its fresh, tart taste, it is a good dessert apple when allowed to ripen on the tree until early April. It is probably our best cooking apple although many people would prefer the Granny Smith. It originated at Sturmer in Suffolk, England about 1843.

DEMOCRAT
This is a large, dark red flat apple with a tough skin and a yellowish, dry, sweet flesh. It keeps very well. Democrats began when a chance seedling was discovered in an orchard at Glenorchy, Tasmania about 1920.

GRAVENSTEIN
The Gravenstein apple is early maturing, medium to large in size, of high quality for both cooking and dessert. It is flattened in shape with white to cream flesh, sub-acid and aromatic. This is an old German variety, thought to have originated in the garden of Grafenstein Castle in Holstein in the 17th century.

GOLDEN DELICIOUS
This popular dessert apple starts off green and ripens to lemon-yellow. Flesh is creamy white, crisp, tender, juicy and sweet. A chance seedling found in West Virginia in 1890, it was introduced commercially by Stark Bros. in 1916.

COX'S ORANGE PIPPIN
The Englishman's favourite apple was raised from a pip by a Mr Cox of Colnbrook near Slough, England about 1830. The Cox grows only in climates suited to it (Tasmania, England, New Zealand and Holland).

GEEVESTON FANNY APPLE
Geeveston Fanny is quite a good keeping, late mid-season dessert and pie apple. The flesh is white to cream, firm, crisp and sweet without being very juicy. In cooking, slices retain their shape.

CROFTON
A round, small to medium size, high quality dessert apple which is late maturing. Crofton's flesh is white, resonably crisp and quite juicy, with a mild sweet flavour.

JONATHON
A good small to medium size eating apple with a white juicy flesh and good flavour. Jonathon is at its best in the shops in April, May and June; selected fruit can be kept in good condition in cool storage until the end of October. Named after Jonathon Hasbrouck, in Kingston, New York, where the seedlings were first discovered in 1828, they are now grown extensively in Australia.

LEGANA
The Tasmanian dessert apple, Legana is a medium to large size late red striped and blushed apple often with a purplish red appearance due to bloom on the fruit. The flesh is white to yellowish, often with a greenish tinge. It is a sweet, crisp, juicy fruit, of very good eating quality.

TASMAN'S PRIDE
The flesh is off-white to yellowish, of mild flavour and having quite low acidity when mature. It is juicy and fairly crisp.

SPARTAN
Spartan is a mid-season medium size red to very dark red dual purpose apple, most noted as a dessert variety. The flesh is white to cream, juicy and sweet with a distinctive flavour when mature.

CLEOPATRA
The Cleopatra (Cleo) is a mid-season green to yellow skinned dual purpose apple being at times sunblushed on the cheek. Its flesh is white to cream, quite crisp, juicy and usually with a pleasant flavour. It started in New Jersey, U.S.A. about 1800, and was first grown in Tasmania in 1870.

GRANNY SMITH
Ideal cooking apple when green, and good eating when ripened to yellow-green. Flesh is white, crisp and very tasty when mature, not so sweet. A long keeping dessert apple, it is on the market for most of the year. The Granny Smith originated at Eastwood, New South Wales in 1868 as a chance seedling from an unknown apple in Tasmania. Today it is Australia's main variety accounting for one third of the total plantings.

JONAGOLD
A Jonathon/Golden Delicious cross, this apple is medium size with sweet tasting crisp white flesh. Golden with red stripes and flecks, it is a good mid season apple that keeps well.

FUJI
A big apple that comes in red or green varieties. The green Fuji is a little tart but good to eat. The red Fuji is a sweet apple with crisp white flesh. Fujis have a short shelf life once removed from control storage.

* * * * * *

more about apples

The apple is probably the most important and widely grown fruit in the world. It has been cultivated in Europe for at least 2,000 years, and was introduced into Britain at the time of the Roman invasion.

Before the 17th century two main kinds of apples were grown in Britain, the costards and the codlins, both green cooking apples. Grafts of good quality dessert apples with a red skin were introduced earlier from France, under the general name of pippin, and from these most of the good modern English varieties arose. There are about 2,000 named varieties of apples, however only a few are important commercially, such as the well known Jonathon, Red Delicious , Golden Delicious and Granny Smith.

Apple growing in Australia dates from the arrival of the First Fleet in New South Wales in 1788. Some fruit trees were brought from the Cape of Good Hope and Rio de Janeiro. Captain Bligh of 'Bounty' fame is credited with the introduction of apples into Tasmania, when a botanist on his ship planted the first trees on Bruny Island in 1792. John Pascoe

The staff at the apple evaporating factory in Franklin with a sample of their product. Drying apple slices using heat from wood fires has been long established at Franklin, and this factory is still operating in the same way, having been re-built recently.

Fawkner is regarded as the father of the apple industry; he established the first apple nursery at Launceston about 1830. The Henty brothers took trees from his nursery to Portland in 1834, and Fawkner on arrival in Melbourne in 1837 planted 2,500 trees in an orchard near to where Princess Bridge now stands.

The first commercial exports were from Tasmania to England in a sailing ship. In 1884 a shipment of 100 cases arrived in excellent condition, and in 1887 the first refrigerated shipment was made. From then on exports grew, reaching 400,000 cases in 1907. One ship, the 'Durham' carried 125,000 cases. By 1971 the industry was exporting annually 7 million boxes of apples in a short shipping season of 15 weeks. Apart from Britain and Europe, major markets include Singapore, Hong Kong and the U.S.A. Today, Australia's apple export trade is about 3 million boxes per season, with increasing emphasis on markets in South East Asia.

notes

Best-selling Recipe Books
from Southern Holdings

The Australian Apple Recipe Book
Includes 148 top recipes, plus orchard photographs and calendar, apple varieties, and historical apples

The Australian Convict Recipe Book
Includes 150 practical recipes, plus historical photographs, convict rules & rations, and the unabridged story of Bessie Baldwin

The Great Australian Pumpkin Recipe Book
Includes 110 pumpkin recipes (including ice cream), plus the Great Pumpkin story, and Growing & Caring for pumpkins

The Australian Potato Surprise Recipe Book
135 top potato recipes for all occasions; the versatility of this universal food is fully explored. Available after March, 1993

The Australian Historical Recipe Book
Join John Caire in exploring Australia's most popular recipes over the years, including some introduced from Europe and Asia. Includes historical photographs. Available after May, 1993

Recipe Books, per copy: $5.95 plus $1.60 P.&P.
(Fundraisers, please enquire about our special offer)

Organic Gardening Seasonal Guide & Calendar
(published annually in September)
Packed with new, useful, practical gardening information each year. Illustrated. Includes international calendar with moon phases, and diary pages to help keep records and plan your garden efficiently. **$7.50 plus $1.50 P.& P.**

Complete Organic Gardening
Our best selling gardening book is a unique guide to better gardening and increased self sufficiency. Beautifully illustrated throughout. **$14.95 plus $2.60 P.& P.**

ORDER BY MAIL, PHONE OR FAX FROM:
**Southern Holdings Pty Ltd. P. O. Huonville 7109, Australia.
Phone: (002)664112; Fax: (002)664112. ACN 009550841 Credit
card orders accepted. All orders sent return mail by Australia Post.**